Writing Research Papers Using Mendeley-A Hand Book

AF497458

Dr.G. Suseendran, M.Sc., M.Phil., Ph.D.,

Assistant Professor,

Department of Information Technology,

School of Computing Sciences,

Vels Institute of Science, Technology and Advanced Studies (VISTAS),

Pallavaram, Chennai.

Published by

Writing Research Papers Using Mendeley-A Hand Book

Copyright © 2018 by Bonfring

All rights reserved. Authorized reprint of the edition published by Bonfring. No part of this book may be reproduced in any form without the written permission of the publisher.

Limits of Liability/Disclaimer of Warranty: The authors are solely responsible for the contents of the paper in this volume. The publishers or editors do not take any responsibility for the same in any manner. Errors, if any, are purely unintentional and readers are required to communicate such errors to the editors or publishers to avoid discrepancies in future. No warranty may be created or extended by sales or promotional materials. The advice and strategies contained herein may not be suitable for every situation. This work is sold with the understanding that the publisher is not engaged in rendering legal, accounting, or other professional services. If professional assistance is required, the services of a competent professional person should be sought. Further, reader should be aware that internet website listed in this work may have changed or disappeared between when this was written and when it is read.

Bonfring also publishes its books in a variety of electronic formats. Some content that appears in print may not be available in electronic books.

ISBN 978-93-86638-90-8

Publication Date: 7th April 2018

Author

Dr.G. Suseendran

Bonfring

309, 2nd Floor, 5th Street Extension, Gandhipuram,

Coimbatore-641 012.

Tamilnadu, India.

E-mail: info@bonfring.org | Website: www.bonfring.org | Phone: 0422 4213231

Preface

The book "**Writing Research Papers Using Mendeley-A Hand Book**" is the fruit of his hard work. It is the handy work that every research students to posses. Dr.G. Suseendran, Assistant Professor, Department of Information Technology, School of Computing Sciences, in Vels Institute of Science, Technology and Advanced Studies (VISTAS), Pallavaram, Chennai. The idea of publishing the book "**Writing Research Papers Using Mendeley-A Hand Book**" dawned in our minds which would be of great benefit to write a research papers using mendely software.

The book is designed to help research scholar to develop capabilities of writing the research papers.

The book contains nine chapters, all the chapter are explained vividly in a lucid manner. An attempt has been made to keep the language as simple as possible and students will definitely be able to appreciate this book.

We hope that this book will be of great help for the students to understand the mendely software which in turn will help them to write the research papers.

Suggestions for further improvement of the book will be thankfully acknowledged.

Dr.G. Suseendran

www.suseendar.com

Acknowledgement

We owe our heartfelt gratitude to respected Chancellor of Vels Institute of Science, Technology and Advanced Studies (VISTAS) Dr.Ishari. K.Ganesh, M.Com.,M.B.A.,B.L.,Ph.D., and Dr.Aarthi Ganesh., Pro-Chancellor (Academic), for providing us with an opportunity to author this book.

A deep sense of gratitude to Dr.A.Jothi Murugan, Vice President (Planning and Development) of Vels Institute of Science, Technology and Advanced Studies (VISTAS) for his rocksolid backing and unstinted support he has given throughout this long arduous venture.

Our sincere thanks to Dr.P.Swaminathan, Vice Chancellor (i/c) for motivating us to move on into the path of innovation and research and publication of books.

We wish to place on record our gratitude to Dr.A.R.Veeramani, Registrar for being a source of encouragement to this great endeavour of ours.

We are very grateful to Dr.P.Mayilvahanan, Director, School of Computing Science, Dr.P.Sujatha, Head, Department of Information Technology, School of Computing Sciences for their kind co-operation and understanding towards us during this heavy task in hand.

We take this opportunity to thank our colleagues for their support and assistance. We thank profusely all those who have helped us in some way or other in bringing out this book.

We thank the publisher for his painstaking effort in bringing out this book.

Any suggestion for the improvement of the book is most welcome.

Dr.G. Suseendran

www.suseendar.com

CHAPTER–I

1.1. Introduction

Mendeley Desktop is a Web-based intelligent system for posting, altering, looking into, and scrutinizing scholastic research. It records and sorts out your papers, PDFs, and different tools into a simple to-utilize interface.

Mendeley online highlights additionally and make it simple to get to work posted by different specialists and also get to scientific, medical, and specialized databases.

Mendeley Desktop requires a free Mendeley account that empowers clients to share and match up information over various PCs and cell phones.

Mendeley is a reference administration tool that gives you a chance to gather and compose references, and then effectively embed them into reports and organization book references.

In any case, it additionally gives you to drag and drop PDFs into your library and concentrates the metadata to make a library.

Like other social networking tools, you can use Mendeley to invite colleagues to share your documents and PDF file of your research papers.

1.2. Mendeley Desktop Interface

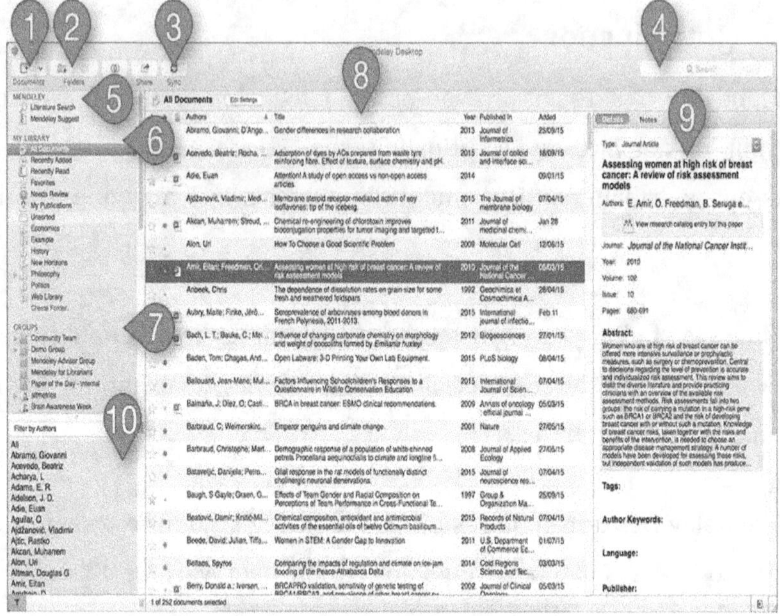

1. **Add files menu** – Add File menu is used to add the PDF document in the Mendeley Software. To add a file select File menu and choose add option.

2. **Folders menu** – Add 'Add folder' button to create a new folder to organize your documents and PDF files.

3. **Sync**. This button helps to updated any changes made in the Mendeley and library. Once you click the button it moves to cloud for storage, making them available on other devices and computers where ever you move.

4. **Search** – To search the information year, paper title, author name in the PDF and documents added in the Mendeley library.

5. **Literature Search**– To seek inside Mendeley's group sourced index.

6. **My Library** – View the whole contents of your own library by choosing 'All Documents'.

7. **Groups** – To create or join any groups in the Mendeley

8. **Main panel** – The Panel display all the documents and PDF files added in the Mendeley Library. To open the document just double click the document on the list.

9. **Details panel** – The detail panels displays on the right hand side which shows the all the information of the document you have selected such as Paper Title, Author Name , Journal Name, Year of Publication, Abstract etc.

10. **Filter panel** – The filter panel offers author filters. It displays author name of the documents added in the Mendeley.

1.3. Mendeley Tool Bar

1. *Text Select Tool*

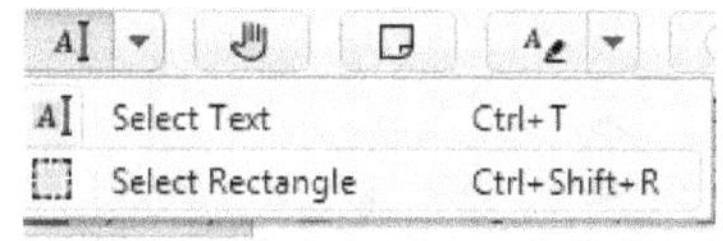

Select Text: Select Text tool is used to select the text by blocking each and every line of the text in the document .It is also used to highlighting the text by using Highlight Text tool.

Select Rectangle

Select Rectangle tool is used to select the text by blocking the paragraph in the document. It is also used to highlighting the text by using Highlight Text tool.

2. *Pan Tool*

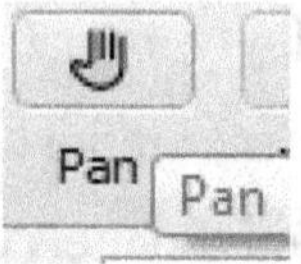

Pan tool is used to scroll around the document. Click the Pan tool to scroll through the document.

3. *Note Tool*

Note Tool is use insert notes in the document to reference. The note tool will appear in whichever color is currently set as active in the color tool. Click the note tool and click on the paragraph a note window appear.

4. *Highlight Tool*

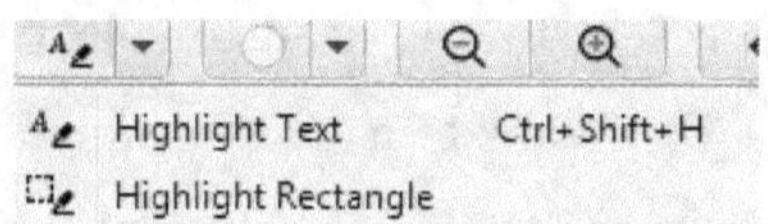

a) *Highlight Text*

Highlight text is used to select the text in the document by blocking the text.

When you select automatically the color changes.

b) *Highlight Rectangle*

Highlight Rectangle tool to select the text by blocking in rectangle of paragraph in the document.

5. *Color Selection*

Mendeley supports highlighting in a number of different colors. Use this menu to select the currently active color.

Notes and highlighting that you apply will use this color.

6. *Zoom*

It is used to view the document Zoon in and Zoom Out. Double click the PDF document you may notice the Zoon Out and Zoom In icon presented in the Tool Bar.

a) *Zoom to Fit- Width*

Zoon to Fit – Width is used to fit the PDF document in Width wise of the document.

This option is used to view the document in horizontal position.

b) *Zoom to Fit- Height*

Zoom to Fit- Height is used to fit the PDF document in Height wise of the document.

This option is used to view the document in vertical position.

7. *Sync*

This button helps to updated any changes made in the Mendeley and library. Once you click the button it moves to cloud for storage, making them available on other devices and computers where ever you move.

8. *General Notes*

General Notes window is use to make notes of the curremt document opened in the Mendeley library. These are not located to a specific position, unlike 'sticky' notes.

Note Tool is use insert notes in the document to reference. The note tool will appear in whichever color is currently set as active in the color tool. Click the note tool and click on the paragraph a note window appear.

9. *Current Document*

Current document is view by Title of the article. Click close tab to close PDF document.

10. *Full Screen*

Full screen is used to view the document in Full screen and it is used to hide the tool bar on full view position of document. To cancel the view press ESC key from the key board to preview the document at normal view.

CHAPTER-II

2.1.   Downloading Mendeley Software

1. Go to Google.Com.

2. Search the key word mendeley software free download and Click search.

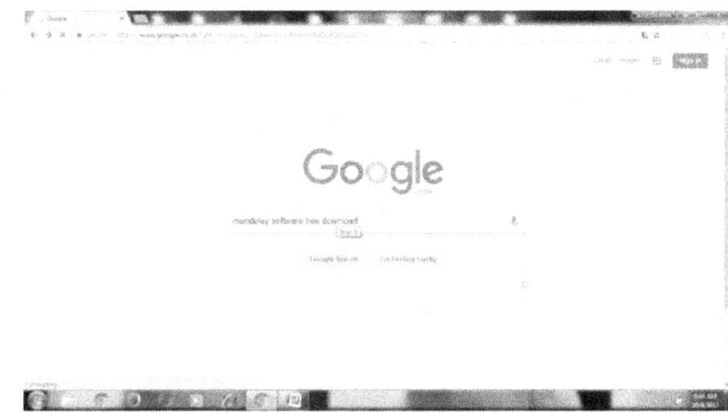

3. The list of option will be displayed by the Google Search.

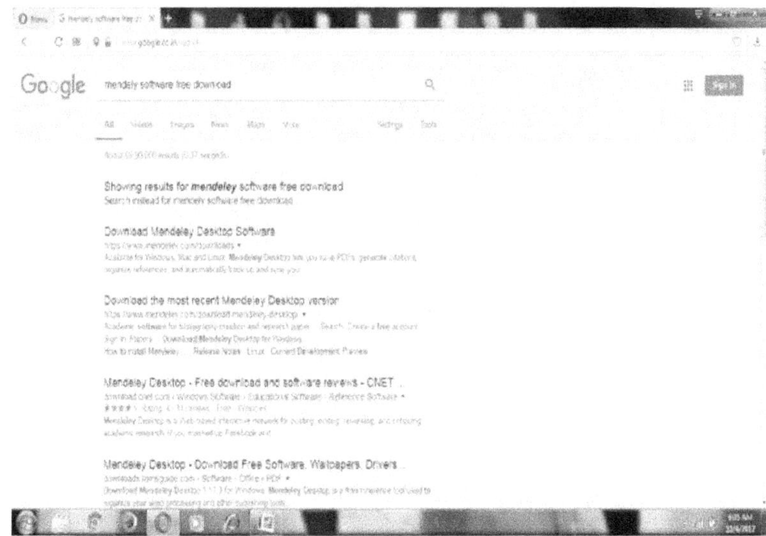

4. Click Download Mendeley Desktop Software

5. It direct to the website of
    https://www.mendeley.com/downloads

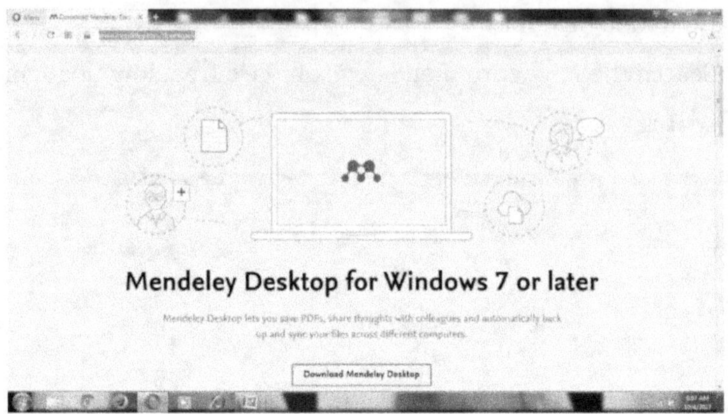

6. Click Download Mendeley Desktop Button to download the software.

7. It displays a screen.

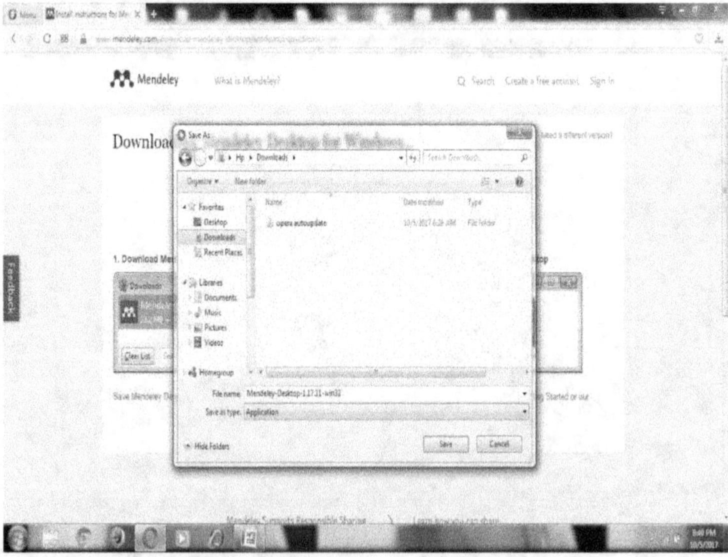

8. Click Save button to download the Mendeley Software.

9. Click the Download load on the Explore as mentioned below or Close the explore Select My computer and double click Download and select the file to install.

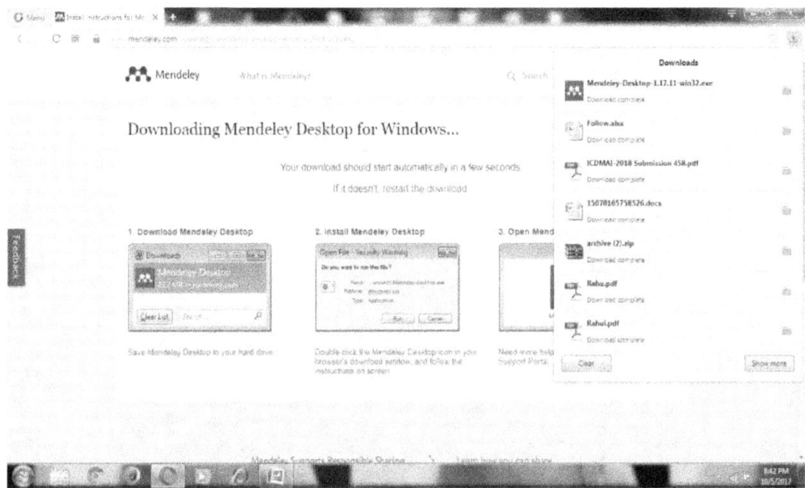

10. Click Mendeley Desk top icon and run the setup, it display the screen as mentioned below.

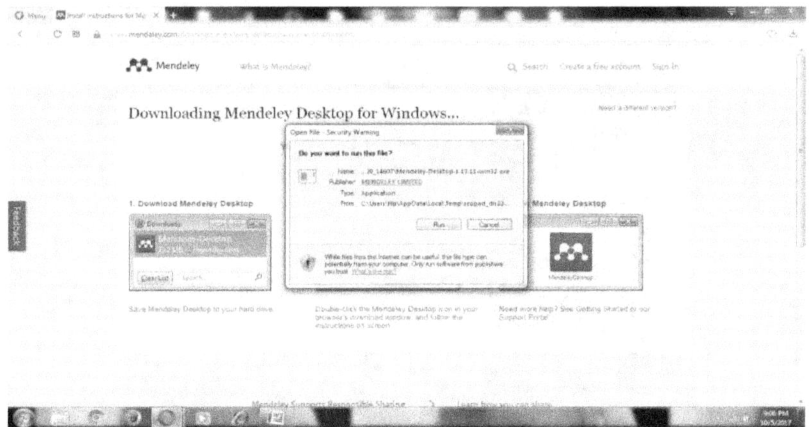

11. Click Run Button to install Mendeley Software it display the
    screen.

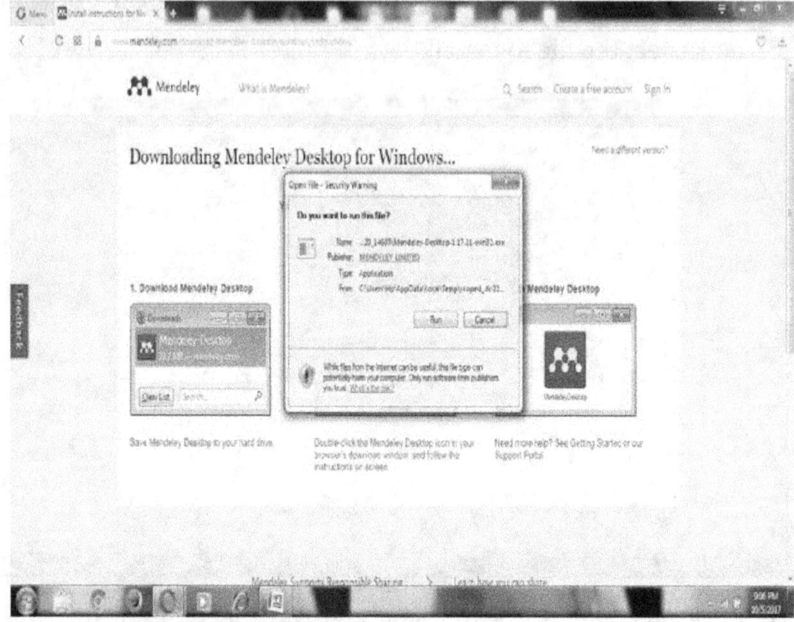

12. It display the screen.

13. Click Next Button to install the software.

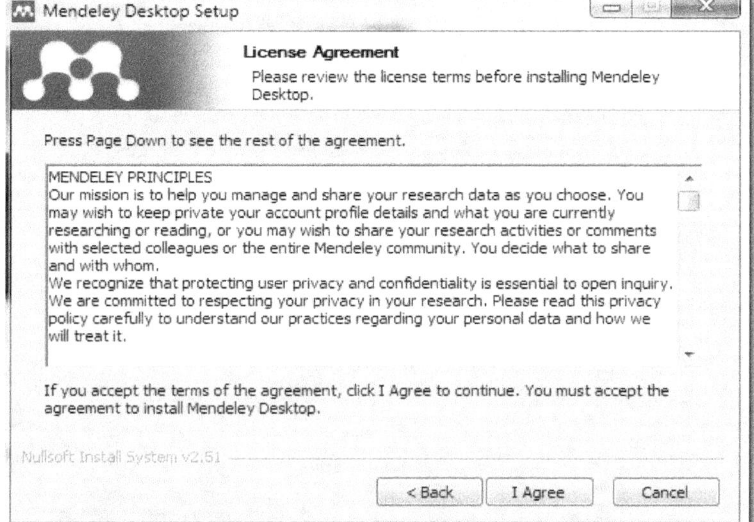

14. Click I agree Button to set the path of file to install.

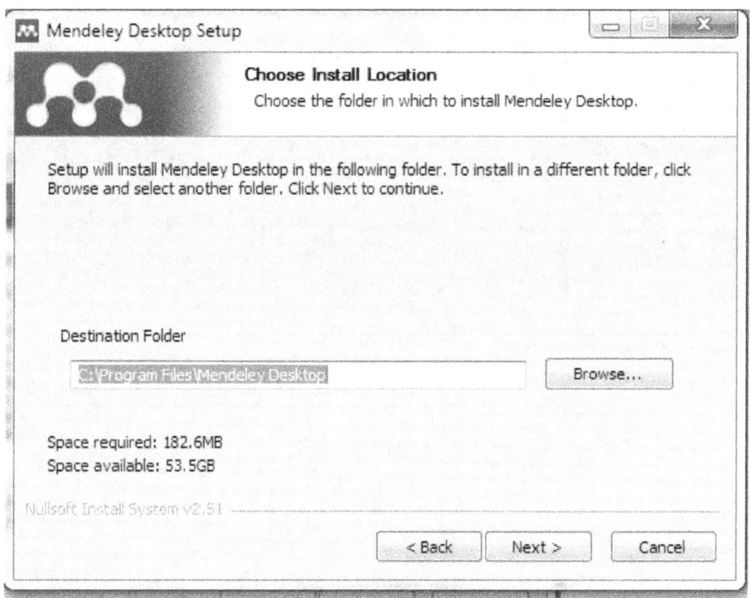

15. Click Next Button to move to next screen.

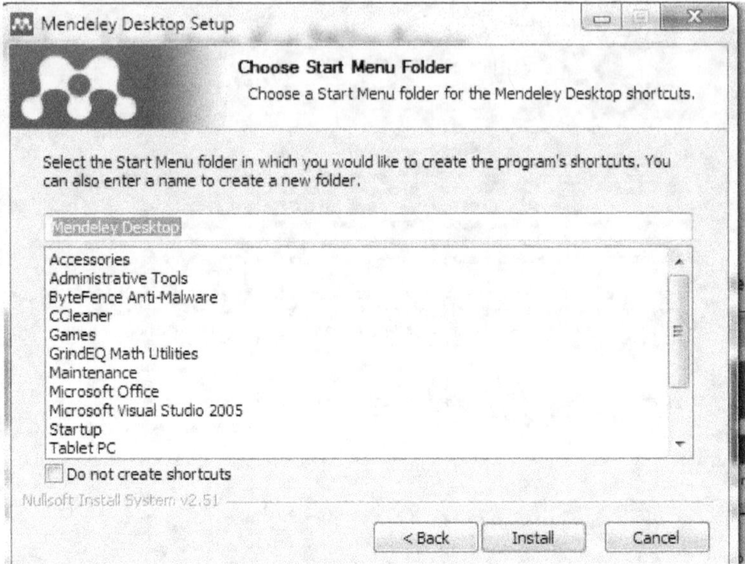

16. Click Install Button to install the Software.

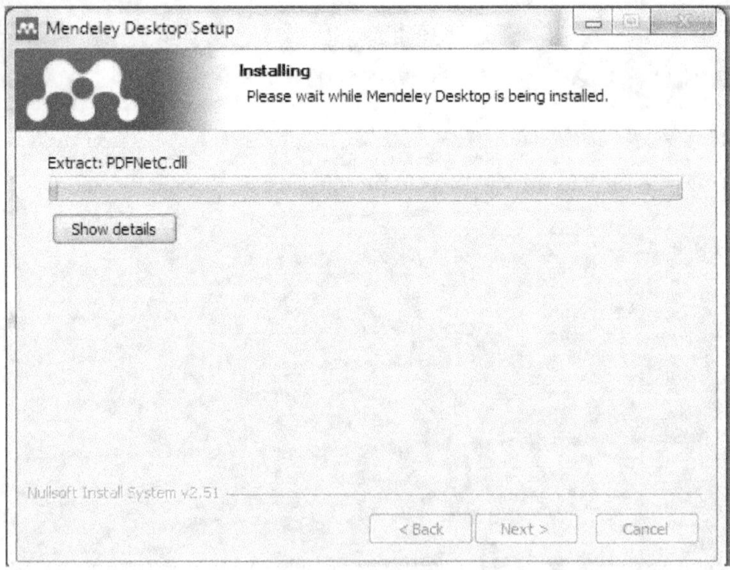

17. After installing it display the screen Click Finish Button.

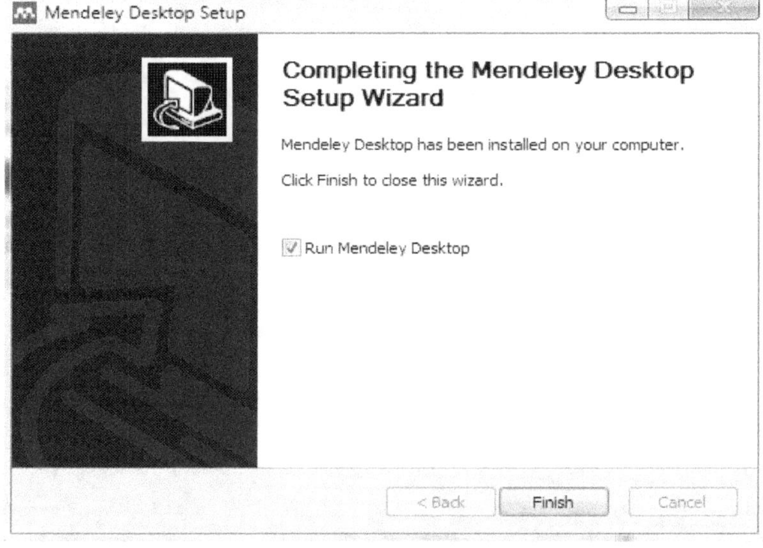

CHAPTER–III

3.1.   Working with Mendeley

1.   Click Mendeley icon on the Desktop to open Mendeley Software.

2.   It display a Screen as below.

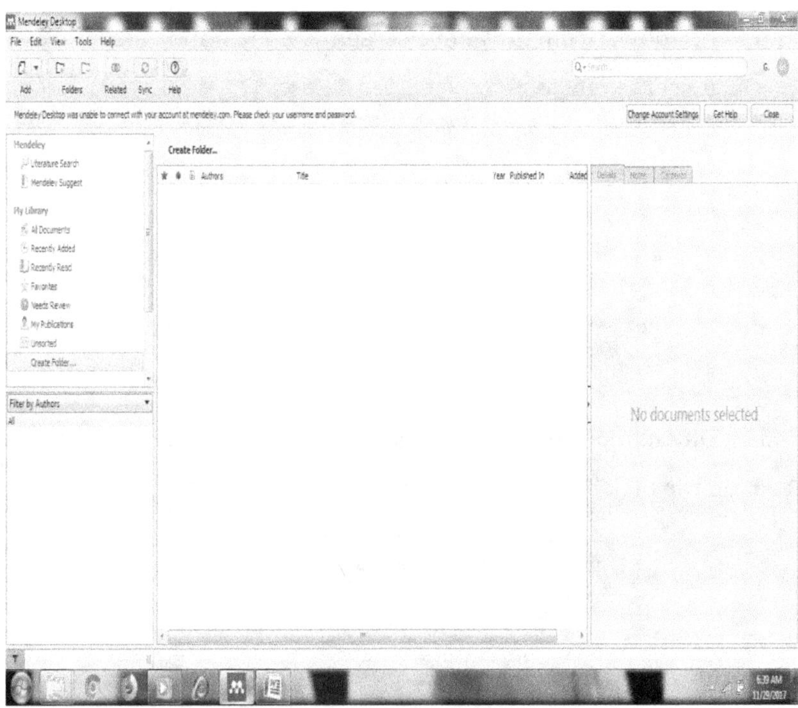

3.2.   Importing Document on the Web to Mendeley

Mendeley Web Importer allow you to import papers, web pages and other documents into the mendely library.

1.   Type www.mendeley.com/import on the web browser.

2.   It display a web page as below.

Mendeley Web Importer

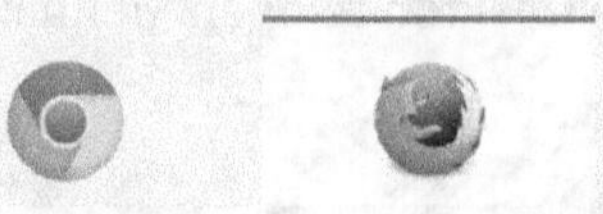

Import papers, web pages and other documents directly into your reference library from search engines and academic databases. Mendeley Web Importer is available for all major web browsers.

3. Scroll down from the above screen you my notice that "Download browser extension".

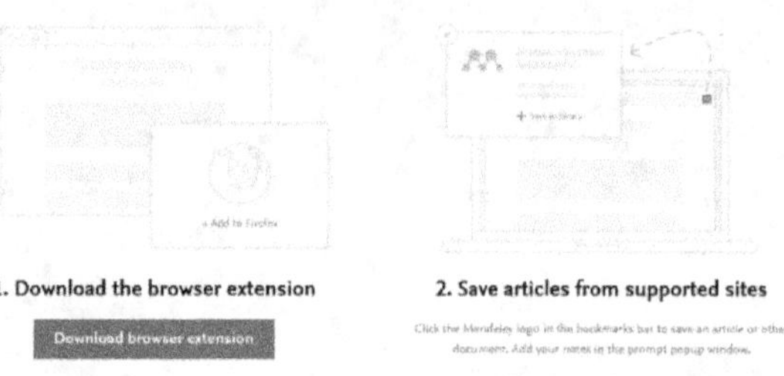

Click Download browser extension and drag to the browser tool and place it on the task bar.

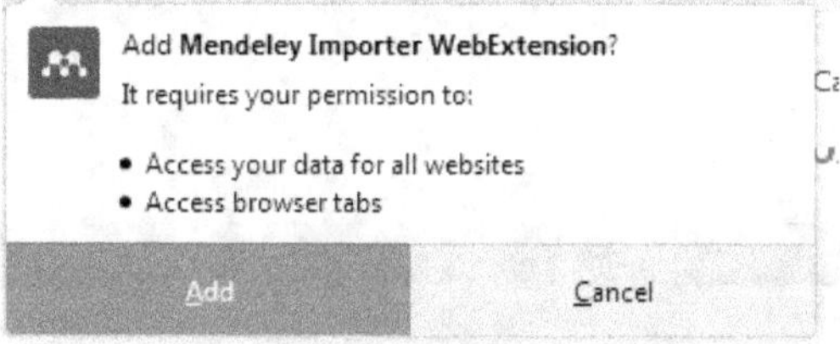

4. Click Add to add the Mendeley Importer on the browser task bar.
5. After adding the Mendeley Web Imprter you may notice the icon will display on the task bar as below.

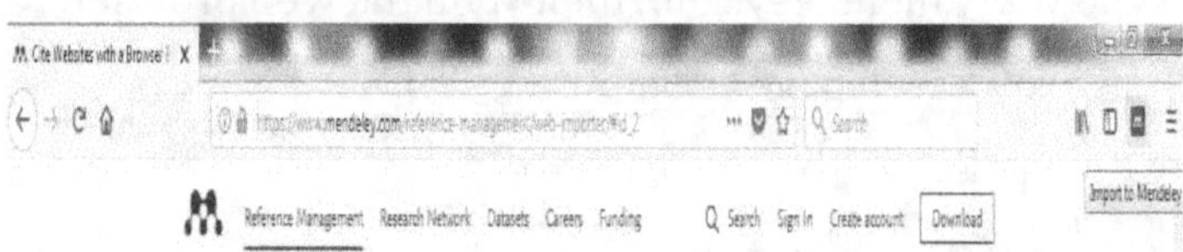

3.3. Inserting MS -Word Plugin

Microsoft Word plugin which allows you to **insert** citations and bibliographies in to your Word document without having to cut and paste or leave Word.

1. Click Tools Menu and Choose **Install Ms-Word Plugin.**

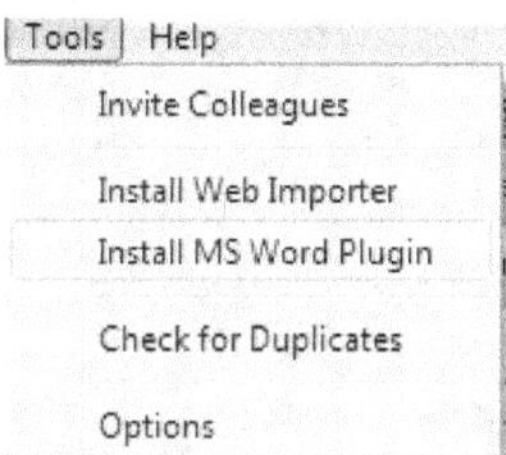

2. Click Install Ms Word Plugin it display as screen.

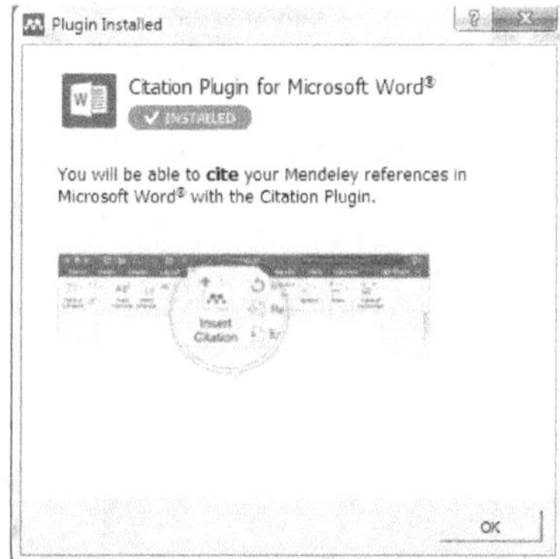

3. Click Ok Button to install Ms Word Plugin.
4. If MS- Word is open back side of your window by mistake it displays a screen as below.

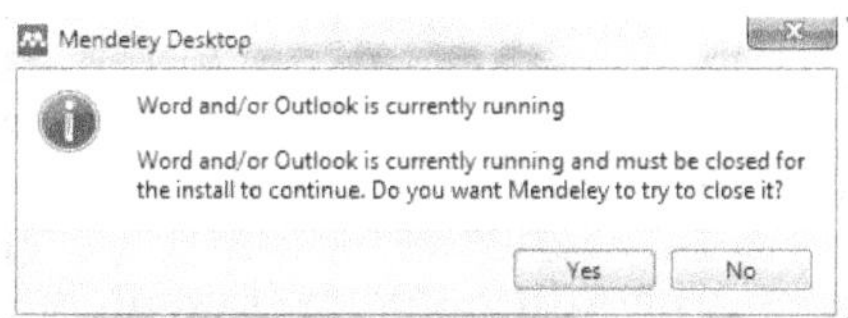

5. Click Yes Button to Install Ms Word Plugin.

6. Open Ms. Word .

7. Click Reference Menu you may notice Mendeley Icon is installed in the Tool Bar.

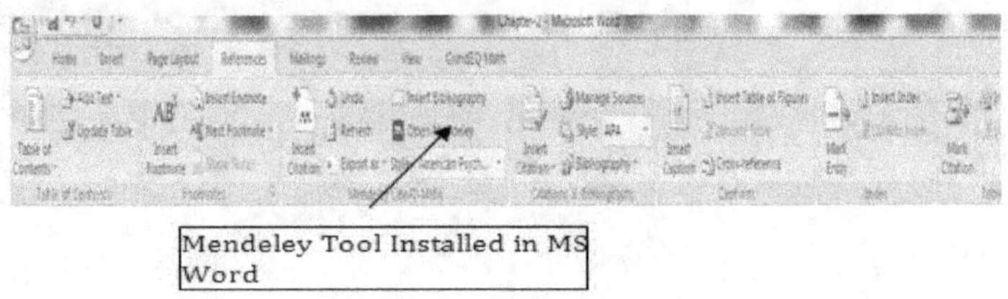

Mendeley Tool Installed in MS Word

3.4.   Creating Folder

Folders are used to categorize and organize references.

Certain **folders** are always present in your **Mendely** library:

1. You can create a folder on the on Mendeley.

2. Click on the Create Folder on the left side of the widow to create a Folder.

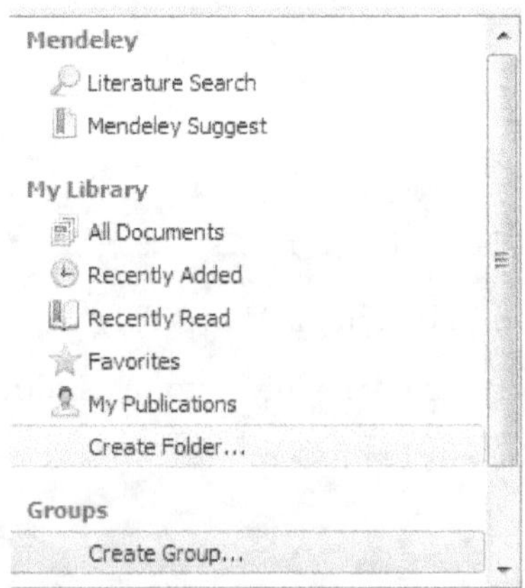

3. Enter the Folder Name as your name eg. "Aditya".

4. Now you can see the **Aditya** folder is created.

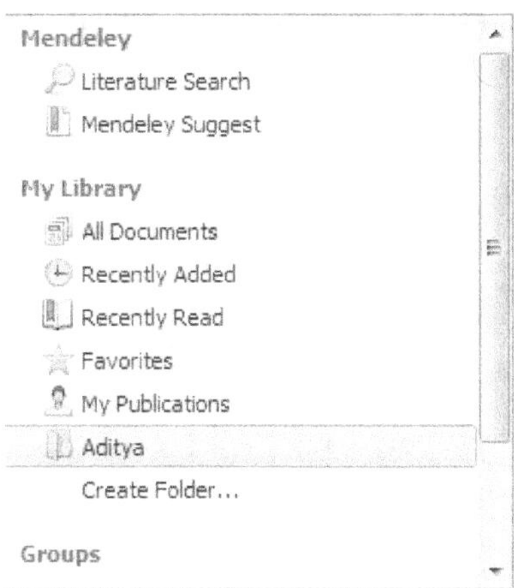

3.5.   Adding Document

1. Adding a document in Mendeley by two methods.

   a) Adding with Menu.

   b) Adding with Drag and Drop.

a) Adding With Menu

   1. Click File menu and Choose Add File option.

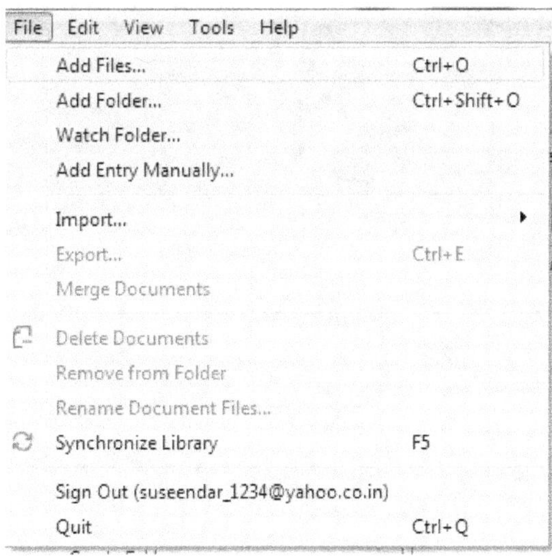

2. Click Add File to add the document it display a screen.

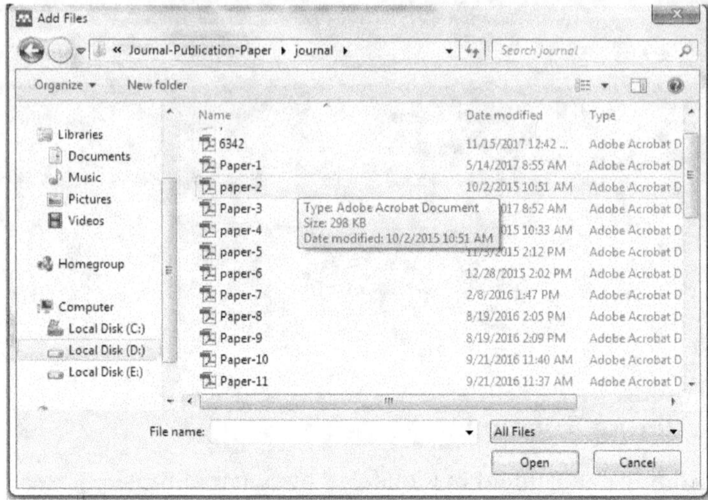

3. Select the Document and click open button to add the document in Mendeley.

4. After selecting the Document you screen will appear as below and you can see the information on the document window.

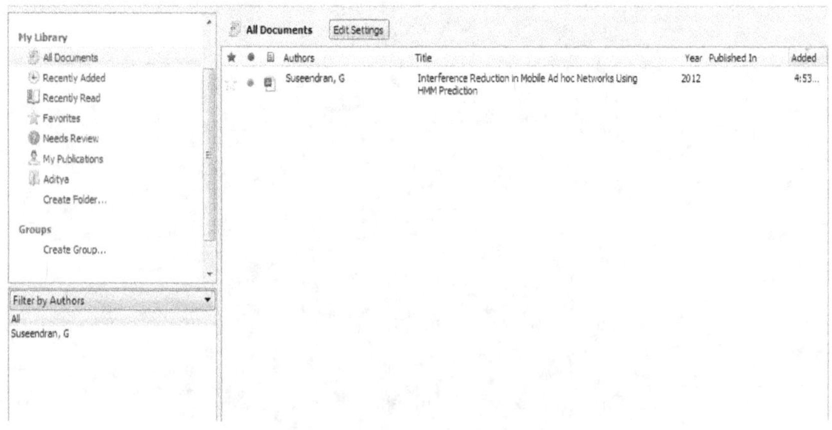

5. You can see Author name title of the paper year of published and published in the document window.

b) Drag and Drop

1. Go the respective drive or your file is in desktop click the document and drag it to Mendeley document.

2. It display as screen as below.

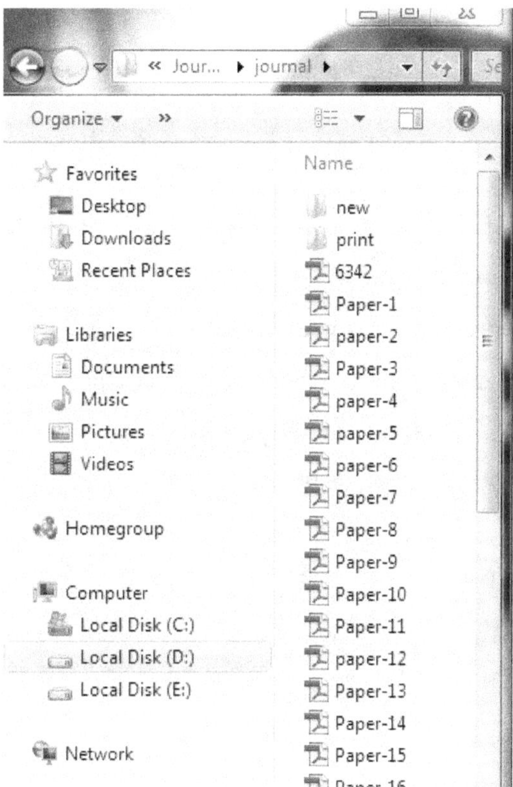

3. Now I am dragging paper two from my D: drive to Mendeley document after dragging the paper 2 you can notice the screen as below.

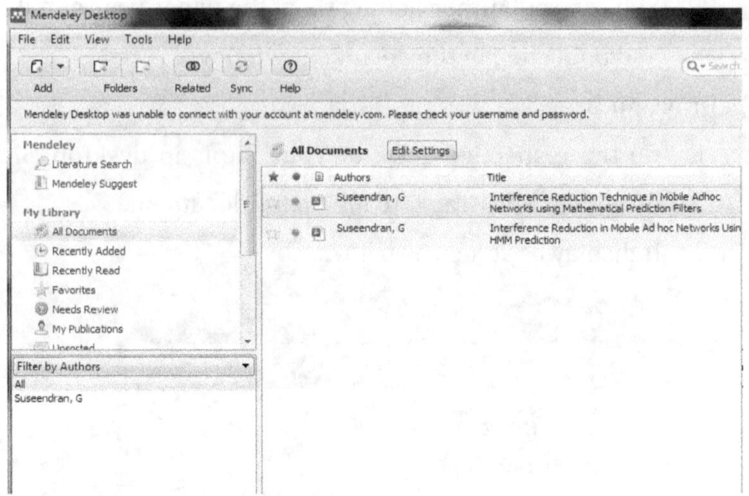

4. After adding the document Click Sync Button to Syncrinze your document to Web.

3.6. Adding Folder to Mendeley

1. Click File menu and Choose Add Folder Option or Right Click Add Folder from the Document Window.

2. It Displays as screen as below.

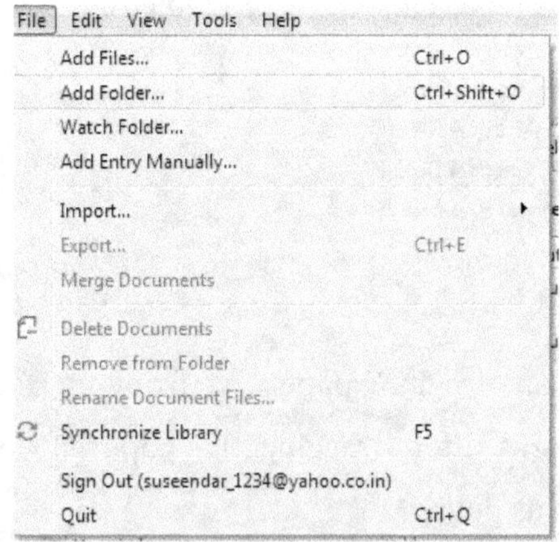

3. After Clicking Add Folder option it display a screen as below.

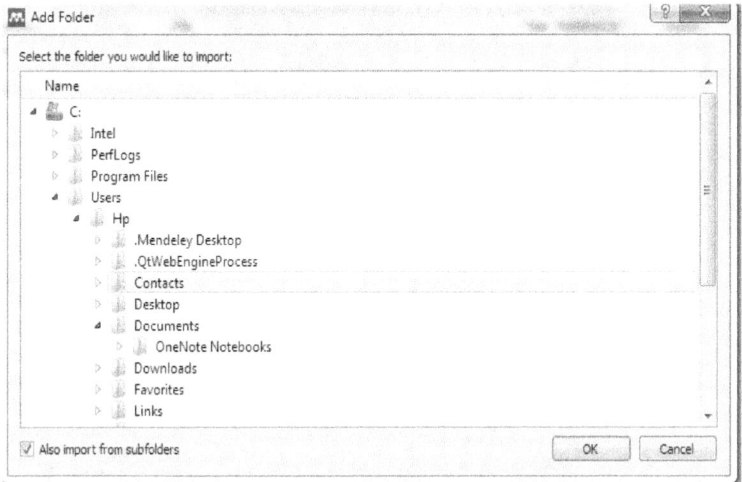

4. Select the Drive in which your folder and click ok Button to add all the document to the Mendeley software.

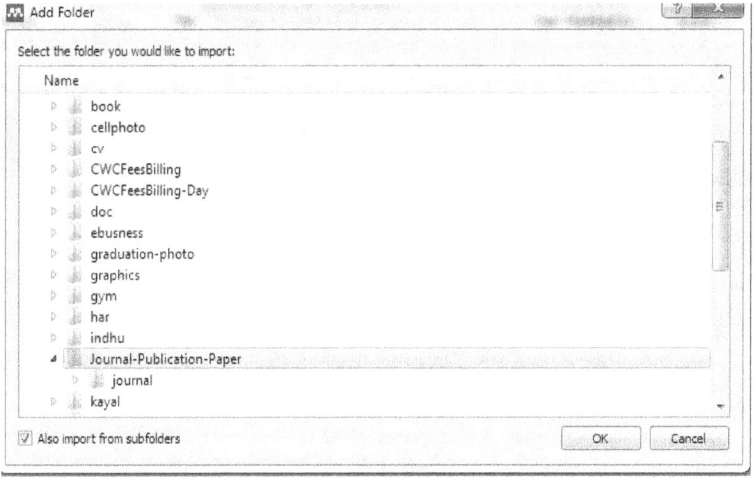

5. Now you may notice all the document in the respective folder will be added as shown in the below screen.

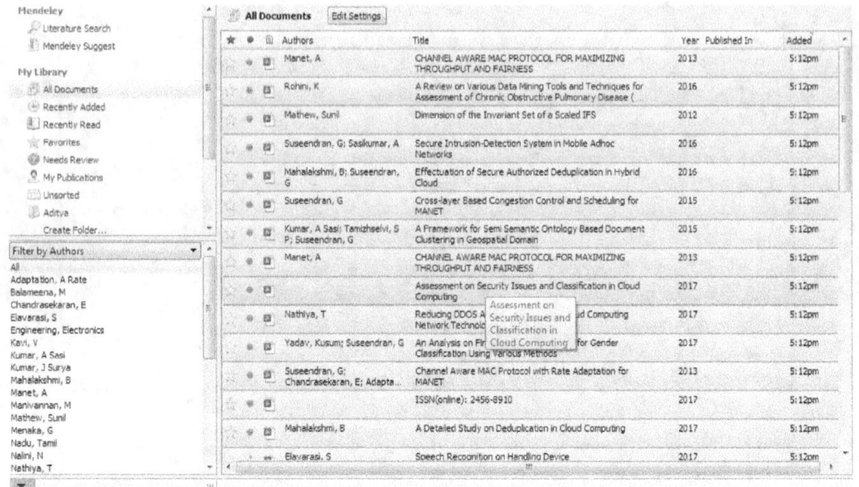

6. After adding the document click Sync all the document on the web.

3.7.   Opening Document in Mendeley

1. Open the Mendeley Software as displays the screen.

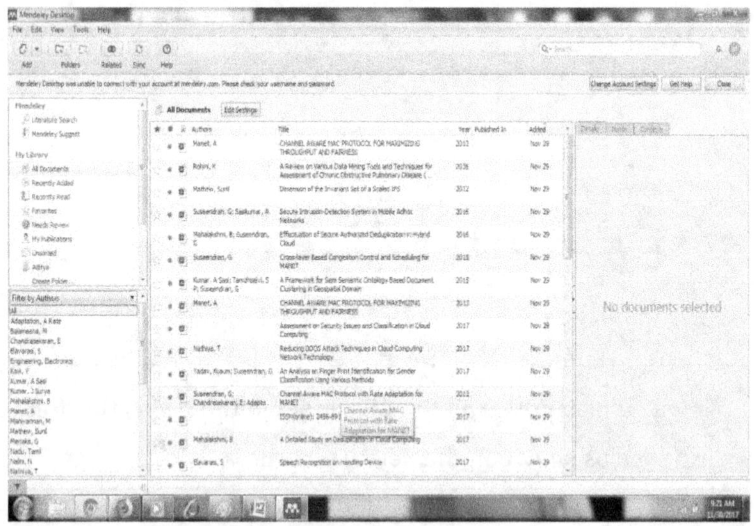

2. Double click the PDF File to open the article to read. It display the screen as below.

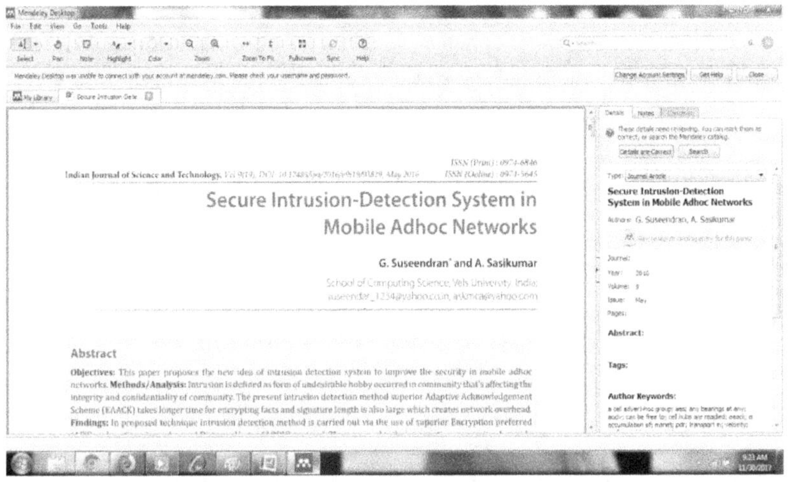

3.8.   Highlighting Text in Mendeley

1. Open the PDF Document by Double Clicking.

2. Block the Text which you need to Highlight as shown below screen.

> Cryptography is the work of art of using so as to achieve wellbeing encoding messages to make them non-meaningful. Its miles a method for concealing data from undesirable client. Cryptography is mulled over a branch of number juggling and pc mechanical expertise. It is far firmly partnered with insights thought, portable workstation security and building. Bundles of cryptography are security of ATM playing cards, PC passwords and electronic exchange, which all rely on upon cryptography[1]. There are sorts of cryptography symmetric key and uneven key cryptography. Figure 1 shows the overview of simple cryptosystem.

3. Right Click with mouse you can find a list from the list menu click Highlight option.

Cryptography is the work of art of using so as to achieve wellbeing encoding messages to make them non-meaningful. Its miles a method for concealing data from undesirable client. Cryptography is mulled over a branch of number juggling and pc mechanical expertise. It is far firmly partnered with insights thought, portable work building. Bundles of cryptograph M playing cards, PC passwords and which all rely on upon cryptography. There are sorts of cryptography symmetric key and uneven key cryptography. Figure 1 shows the overview of simple cryptosystem.

4. After Clicking Highlight option you can notice the block text is highlighted in color as displayed below.

Cryptography is the work of art of using so as to achieve wellbeing encoding messages to make them non-meaningful. Its miles a method for concealing data from undesirable client. Cryptography is mulled over a branch of number juggling and pc mechanical expertise. It is far firmly partnered with insights thought, portable workstation security and building. Bundles of cryptography are security of ATM playing cards, PC passwords and electronic exchange, which all rely on upon cryptography[4]. There are sorts of cryptography symmetric key and uneven key cryptography. Figure 1 shows the overview of simple cryptosystem.

5. To delete the Highlighted Text Right Click and Choose **Delete Highlight** option.

3.9.   Inserting Note

1. Highlight text and Right click on the Highlighted text. It displays as below.

2. Click **Add Note** option it displays a window to annotate the highlighted text.

3. Enter the Note for your reference as below.

4. After adding the note click on the document or click note button on the tool bar to close the note.

5. You may notice an icon will be displayed on the highlighted text.

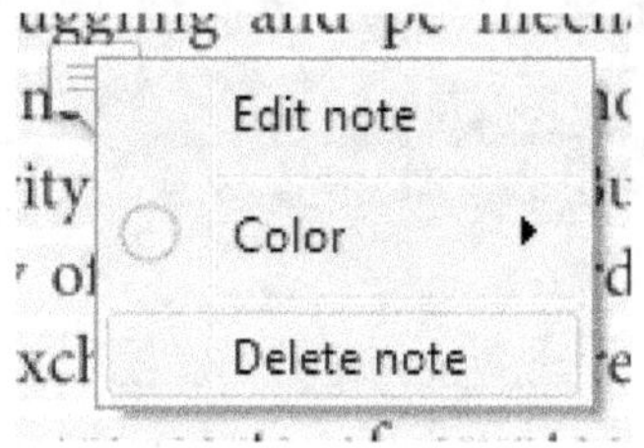

6. Remove the note Right Click on the note icon a popup menu will appear and choose delete note option to delete the note

CHAPTER–IV

4.1.   Annotation

1. Open the Mendeley Software and double click the PDF from the Mendeley Library.

2. Block the text you want to mark annotation as given below.

3. Right Click the selected text and click Highlight option to highlight option.

4. After clicking Highlight option lick **Add Note**. You may find a Note pop up window opens as displayed below.

5. Enter the text as "In MANET Node moves freely and organize the network scalable" in the Note Popup window to annotate as displayed below.

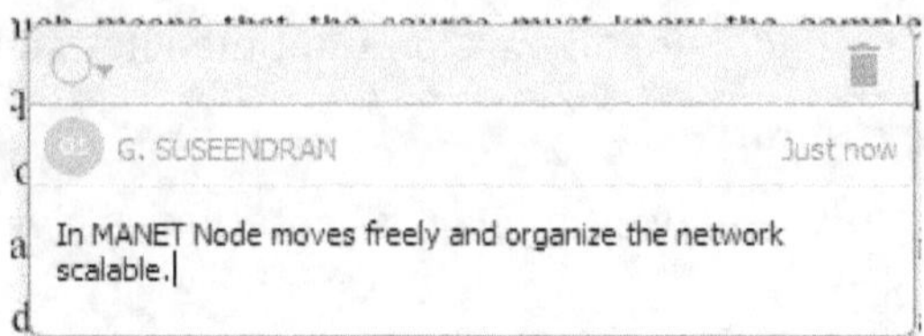

6. Now Click File Menu choose **Export PDF with Annotations** option.

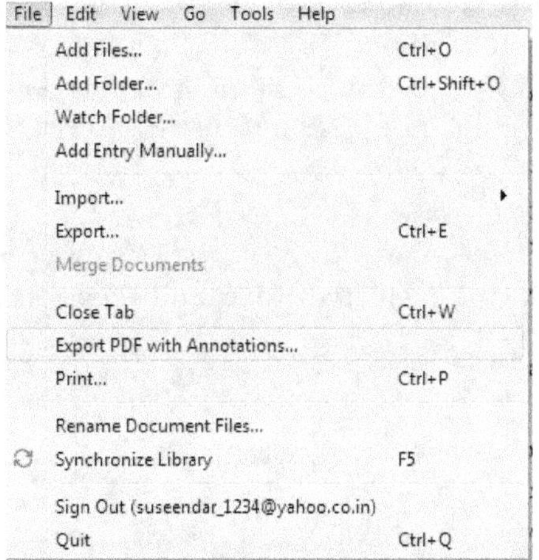

7. It displays a Pop up Window as shown below.

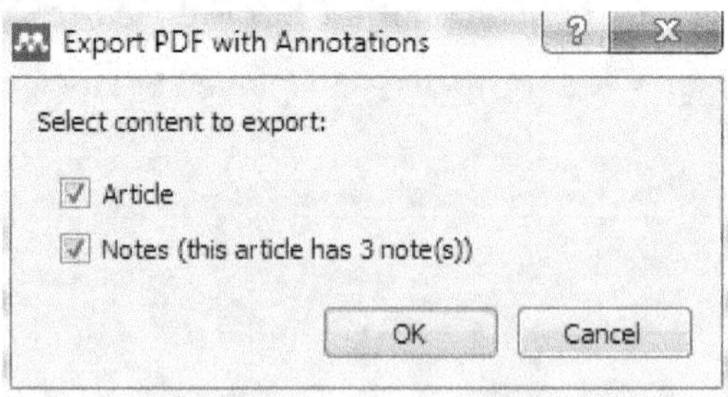

8. Remove the tick mark of **Article** Check Box to de-select the option as shown below.

Note: If both are selected it download the PDF with marked Annotate.

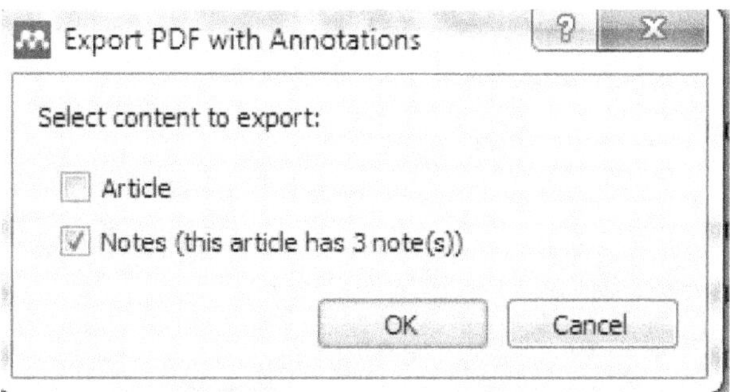

9. Now Click **OK** Button, it displays a Save Pop up window to save the Annotation PDF as display below, Enter the File name as **Annotate-MANET** and click Save Button.

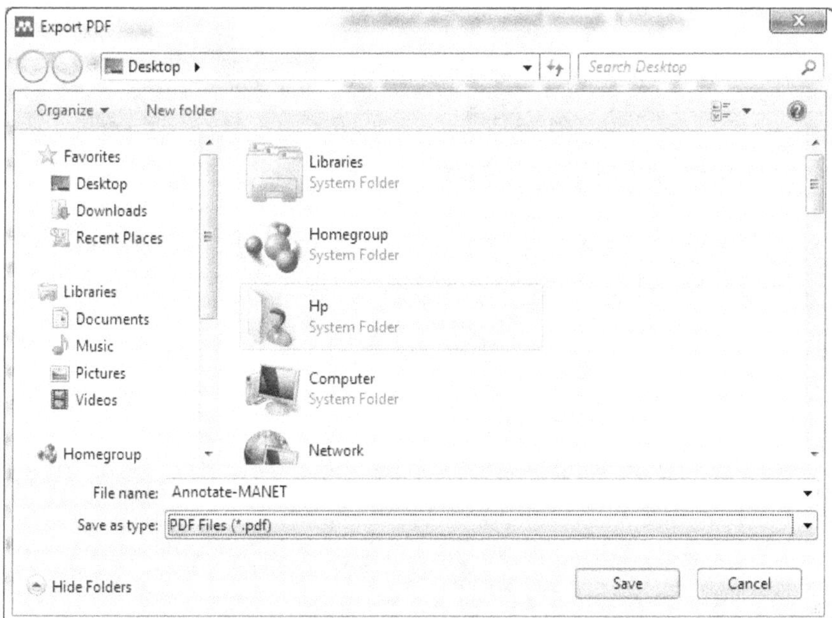

10. Now Click Save Button to Save the PDF.

11. Now Open the Save Annotate-MANET.PDF file from the Desktop.

12. You may notice the PDF file with Annotations as displayed below.

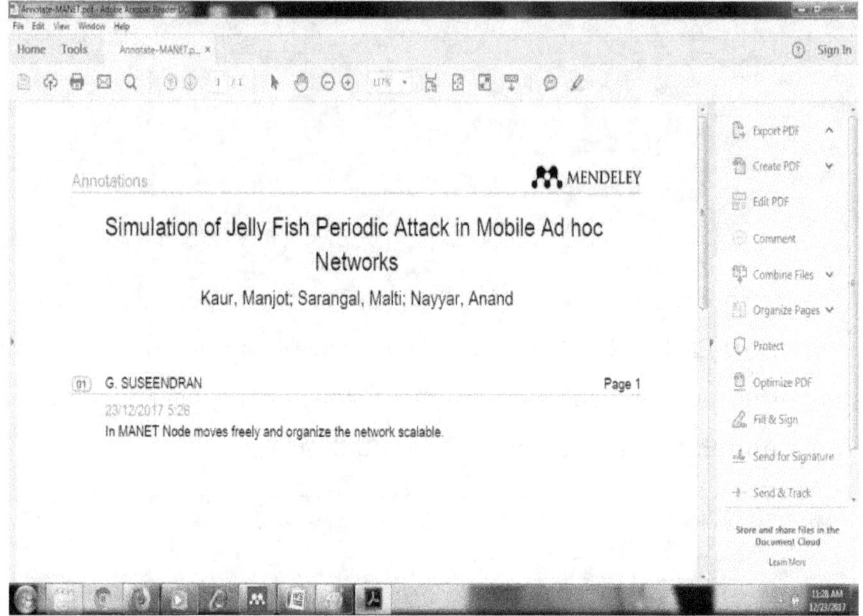

4.2.   Multiple Annotations

1.   Open the PDF and block the text u want to highlight and annotate.

2.   Block the contents and choose highlight.

3. Click Highlight and Add Note it display a Pop up Window enter the Annotate as mentioned below.

4. Now Click File Menu choose **Export PDF with Annotations** option.

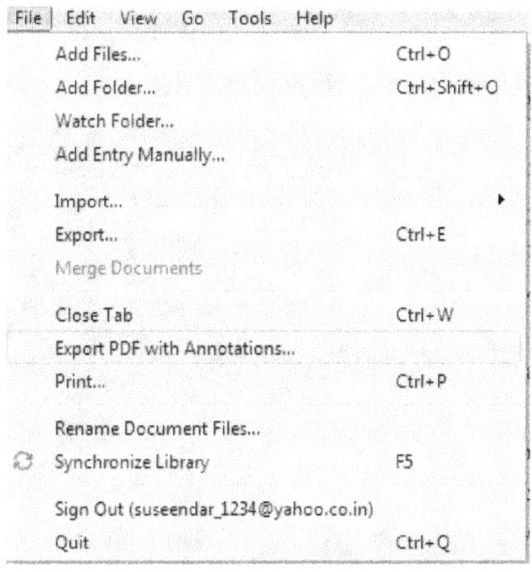

5. It displays a Pop up Window as shown below.

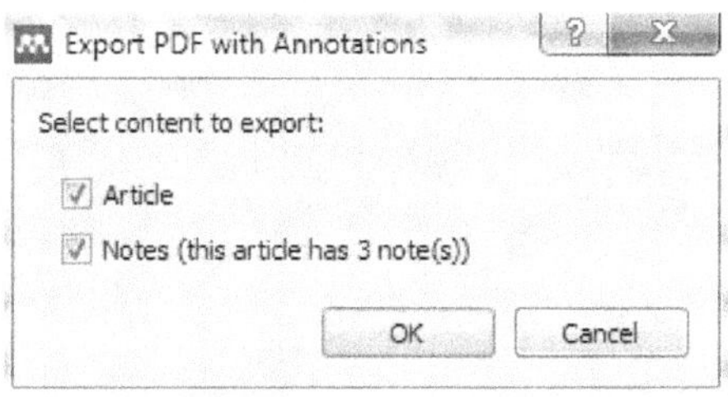

6. Remove the tick mark of **Article** Check Box to de-select the option as shown below.

Note: If both are selected it download the PDF with marked Annotate.

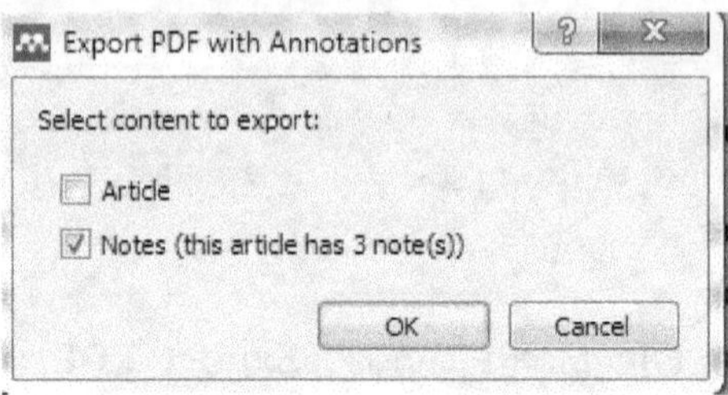

7. Now Click **OK** Button, it displays a Save Pop up window to save the Annotation PDF as display below, Enter the File name as **Annotate-MANET** and click Save Button.

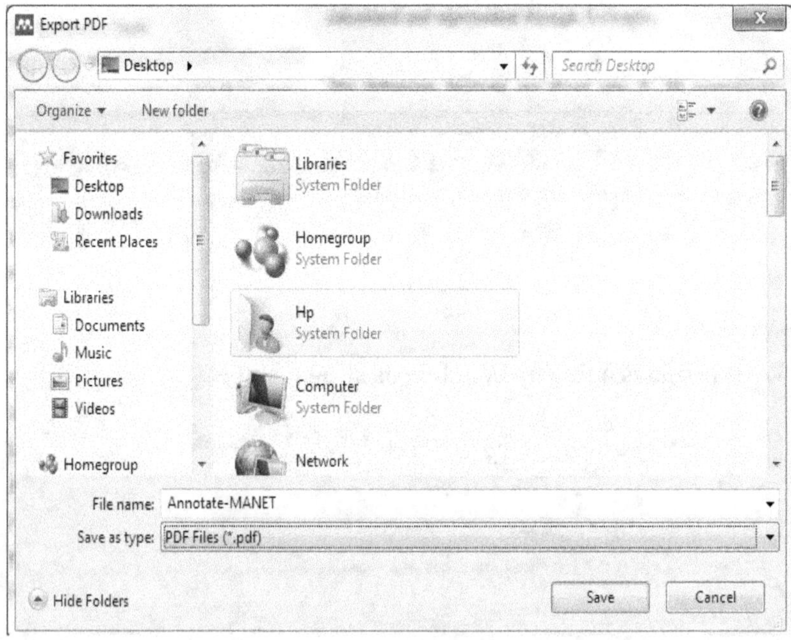

8. Now Click Save Button to Save the PDF. It displays a Message to overwrite the file click Save button to overwrite the existing file.

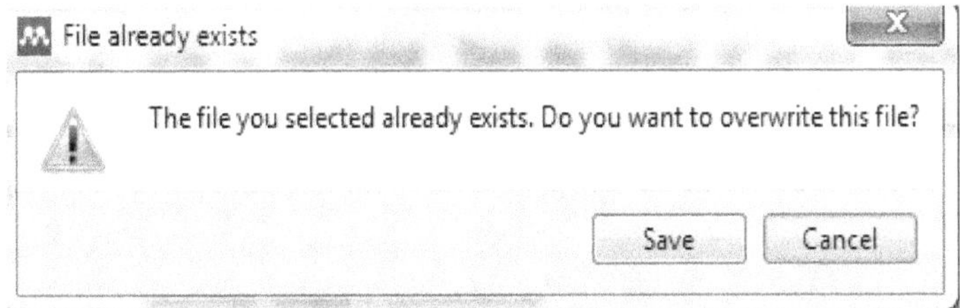

9. Now Open the Save Annotate-MANET.PDF file from the Desktop. It display the PDF as given below.

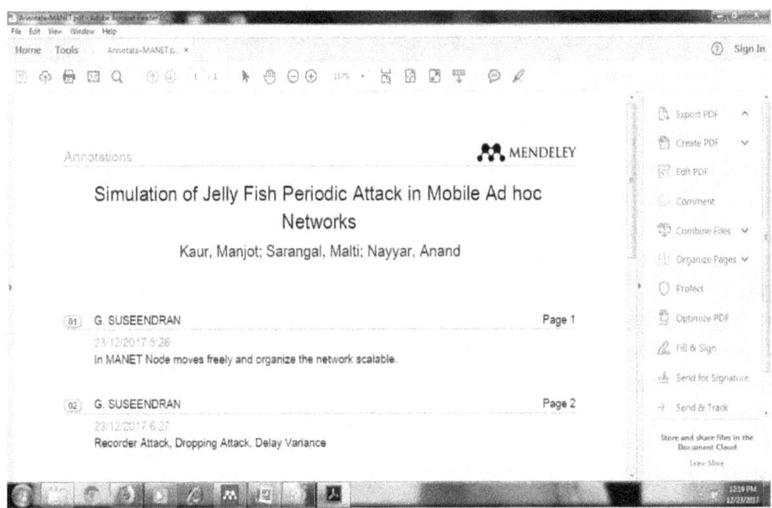

CHAPTER–V

5.1. Generating Citation

1. Open Ms-Word and Mendeley software.

2. Double click the PDF File from the Mendeley Software to extract the text to MS-Word.

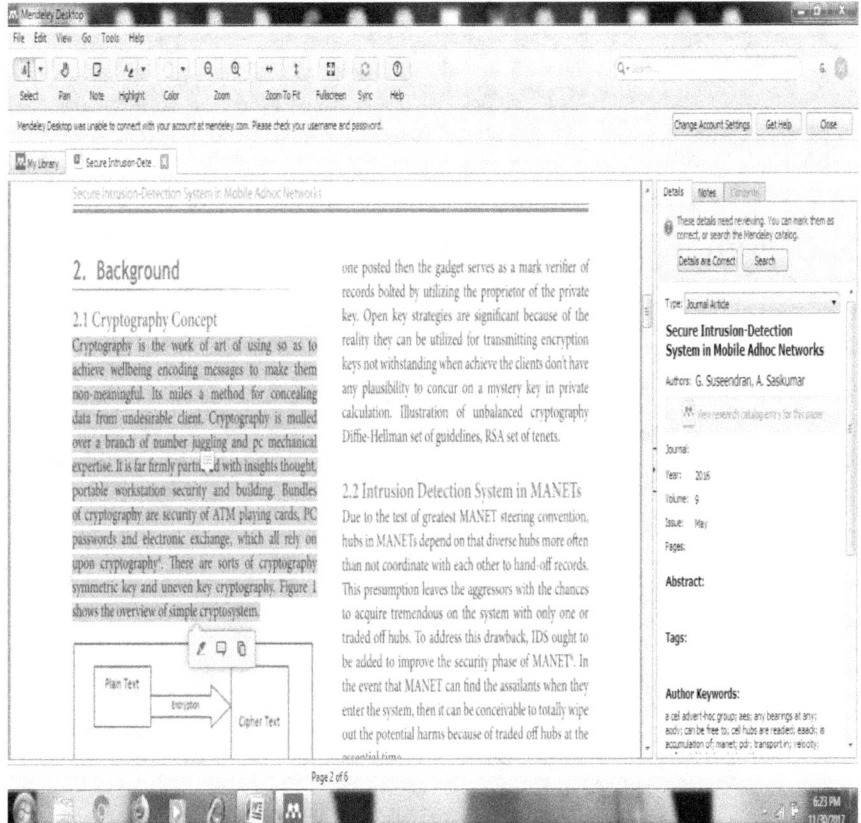

3. Block the Paragraph you want from the PDF file and paste it on MS-Word.

4. Align the pasted document in MS-Word (Line Spacing Justify etc).

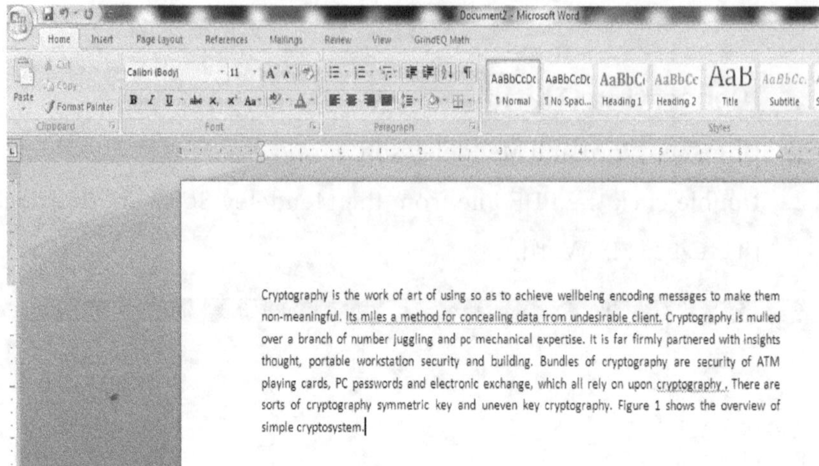

5. Click **Reference Menu** on Ms-Word. It display a Tool bar as shown below.

Citation Icon

6. Click Insert Citation Icon on the tool bar it display a screen as below.

7. Click Go To Mendeley Button to open Mendeley software.

8. Click Cite Button the Mendeley software to cite the reference of the paragraph you have pasted in Ms-Word.

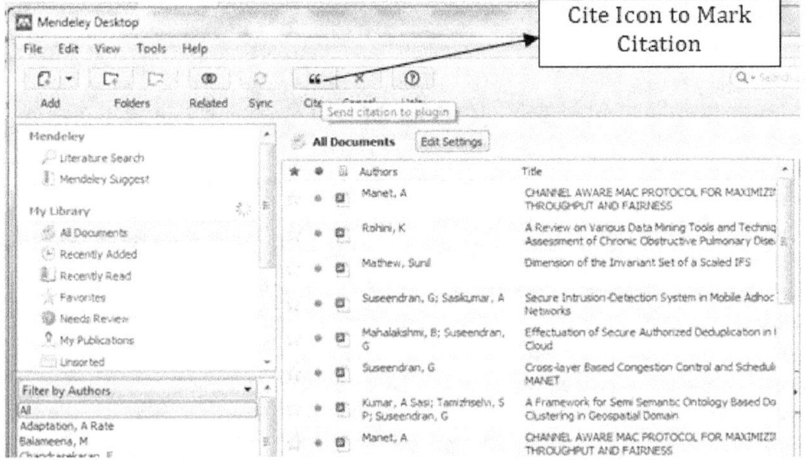

9. After Clicking Cite Button you notice in Ms-Word the author name was added in the end of the paragraph. As shown in the below screen.

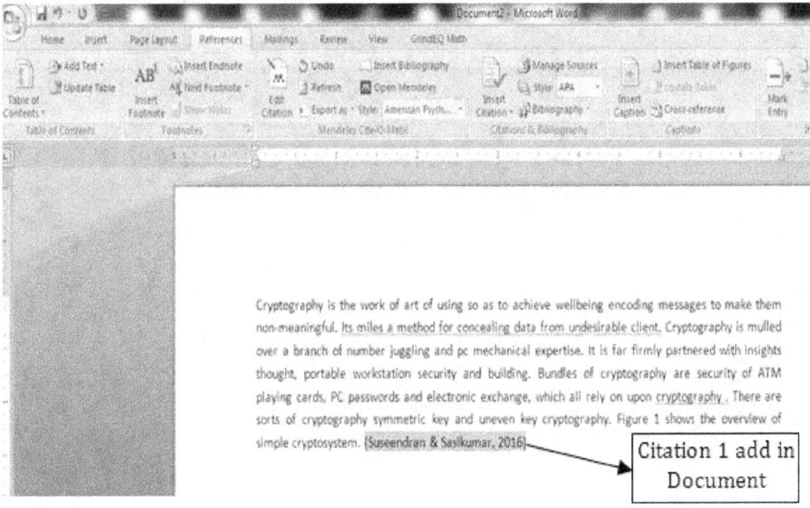

10. Now Double click another document you want to paste in MSWord of related article pdf in Mendeley Software.

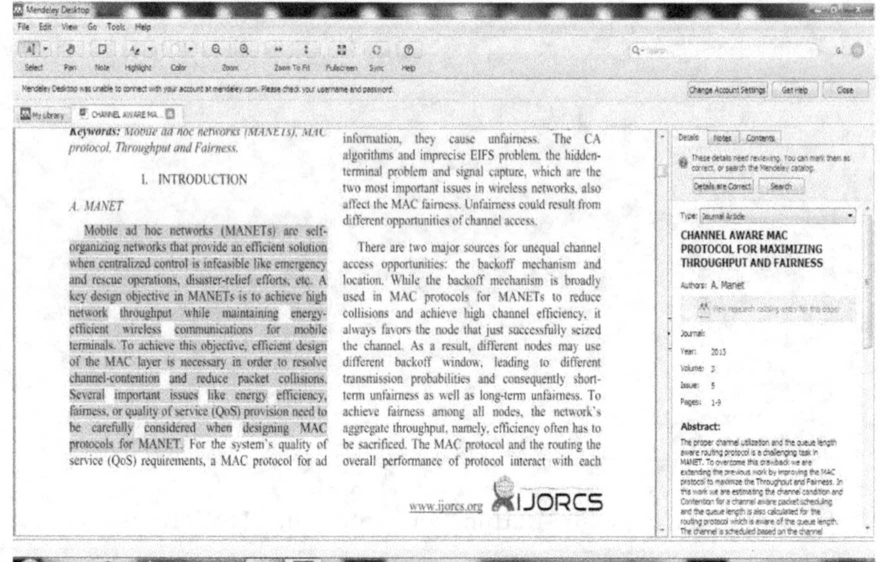

11. Copy the Blocked text and paste in MS- Word (align the document) as the second paragraph as displayed below.

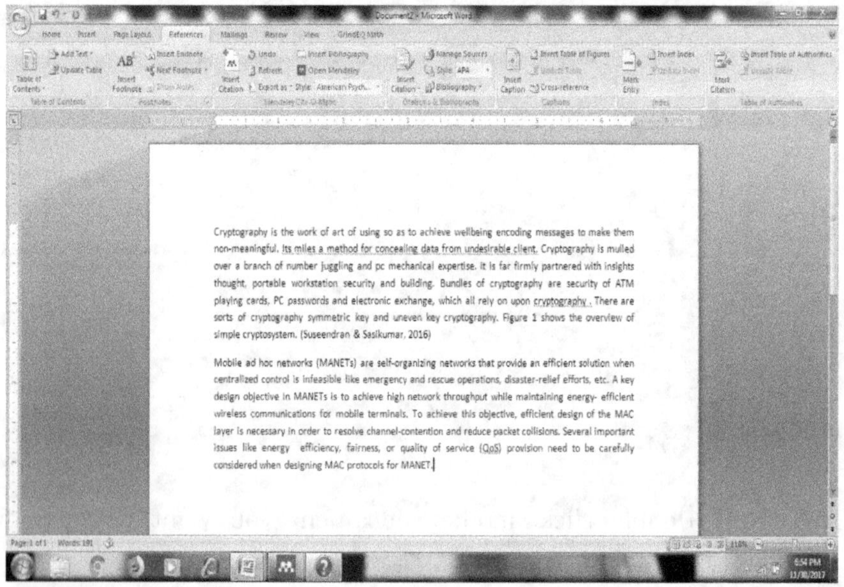

12. Place the cursor on the end of second paragraph.

13. Click Reference Menu and choose Insert Citation Option (follow the steps 6 7 and 8) to mark citation of second paragraph.

14. After repetition of steps you may find the screen as below.

15. Press Enter key on next Line of MS- Word to copy the content from another document.

16. Double Click another document of PDF from Mendeley Software and Block the selected paragraph to paste in MS- Word as displayed below.

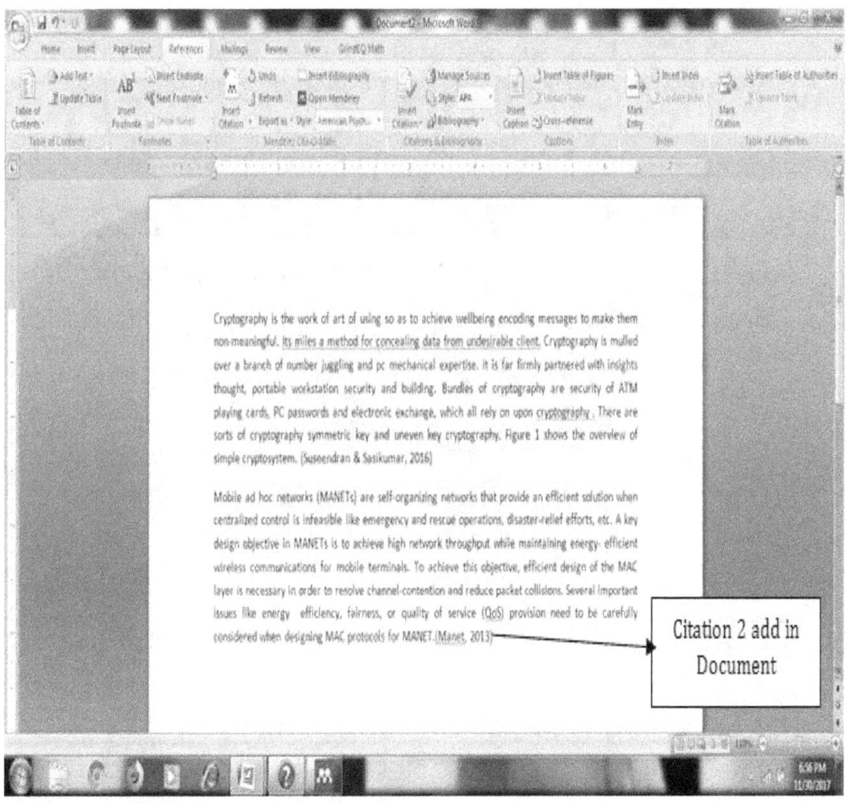

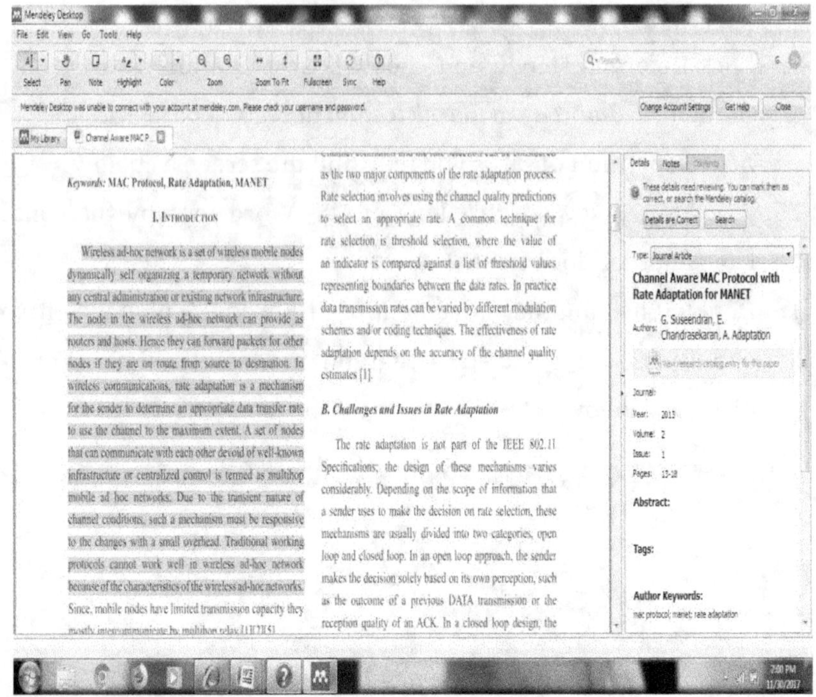

17. Paste the selected text on MS- Word and align the paragraph as displayed below.

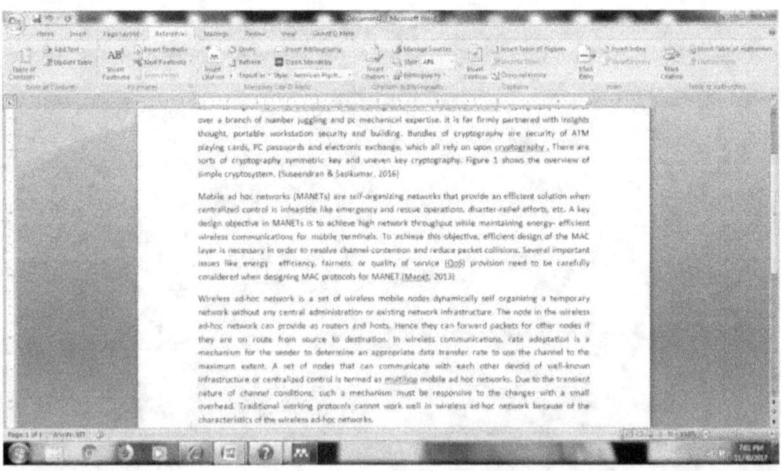

18. Place the cursor on the end of third paragraph and repeat the steps (6 7 and 8) to insert the citation of the document.

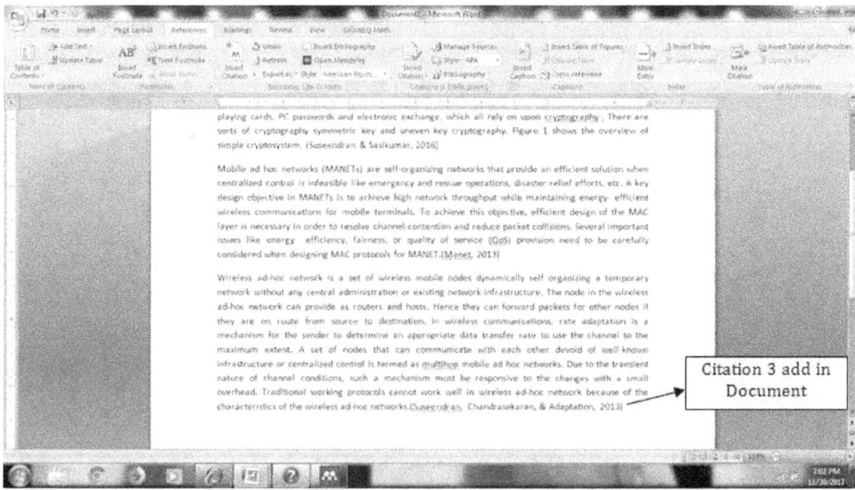

5.2.   Inserting Bibliography

1. To inert the reference Mendeley Type **Reference** on the End of Paragraph as shown below.

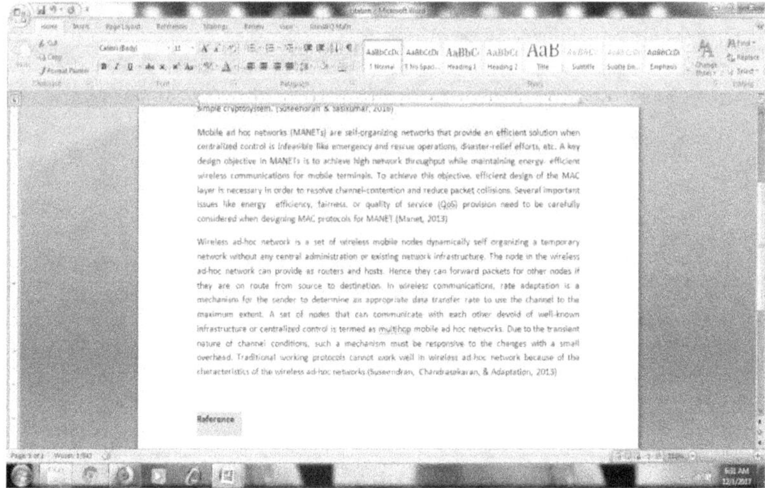

2. Click Reference Menu in the MS-Word Tool Bar and Click Bibliography icon on the Tool bar.

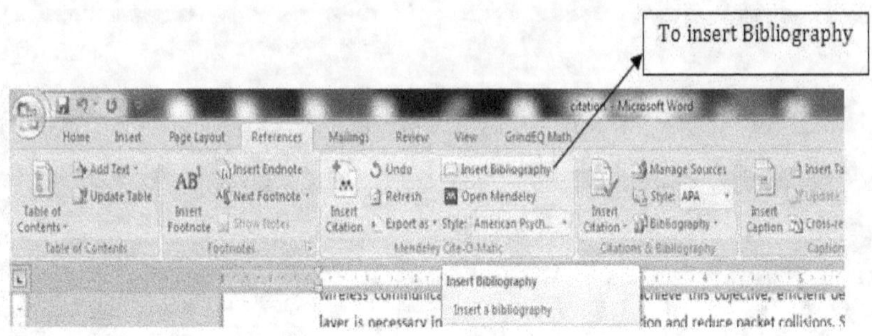

3. You may notice that the reference are added automatically one by one as displayed below.

network without any central administration or existing network infrastructure. The node in the wireless ad-hoc network can provide as routers and hosts. Hence they can forward packets for other nodes if they are on route from source to destination. In wireless communications, rate adaptation is a mechanism for the sender to determine an appropriate data transfer rate to use the channel to the maximum extent. A set of nodes that can communicate with each other devoid of well-known infrastructure or centralized control is termed as multihop mobile ad hoc networks. Due to the transient nature of channel conditions, such a mechanism must be responsive to the changes with a small overhead. Traditional working protocols cannot work well in wireless ad-hoc network because of the characteristics of the wireless ad-hoc networks.(Suseendran, Chandrasekaran, & Adaptation, 2013)

Reference

Manet, A. (2013). CHANNEL AWARE MAC PROTOCOL FOR MAXIMIZING THROUGHPUT AND FAIRNESS, 3(5), 1–9. https://doi.org/10.7815/ijorcs.

Suseendran, G., Chandrasekaran, E., & Adaptation, A. R. (2013). Channel Aware MAC Protocol with Rate Adaptation for MANET, 2(1), 13–18.

Suseendran, G., & Sasikumar, A. (2016). Secure Intrusion-Detection System in Mobile Adhoc Networks, 9(May). https://doi.org/10.17485/ijst/2016/v9i19/93829

4. To Change the style of Reference Click Style drop down list as shown below.

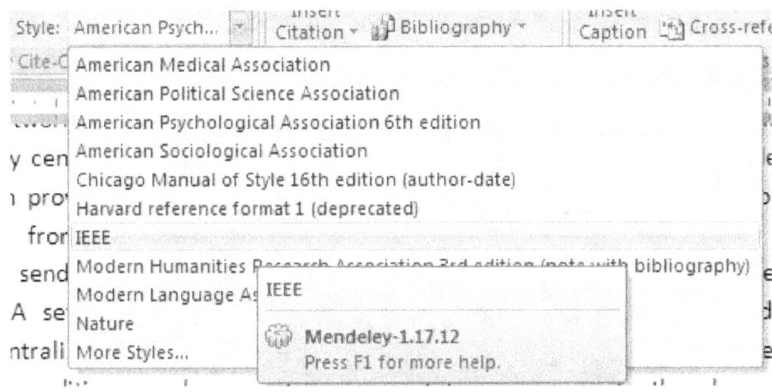

5. Select IEEE to format the reference on IEEE format. Now your reference automatically formatted as below.

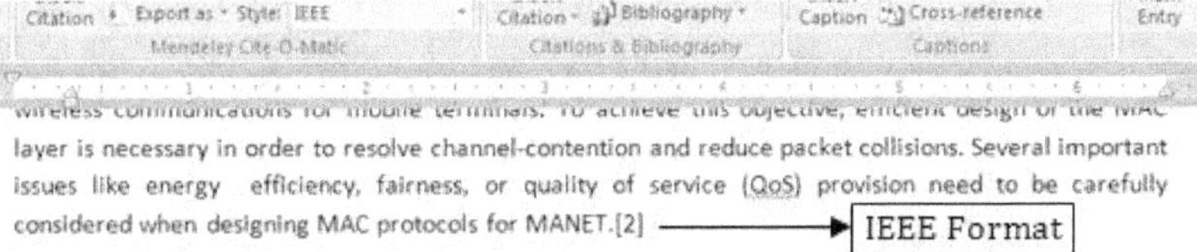

layer is necessary in order to resolve channel-contention and reduce packet collisions. Several important issues like energy efficiency, fairness, or quality of service (QoS) provision need to be carefully considered when designing MAC protocols for MANET.[2]

Wireless ad-hoc network is a set of wireless mobile nodes dynamically self organizing a temporary network without any central administration or existing network infrastructure. The node in the wireless ad-hoc network can provide as routers and hosts. Hence they can forward packets for other nodes if they are on route from source to destination. In wireless communications, rate adaptation is a mechanism for the sender to determine an appropriate data transfer rate to use the channel to the maximum extent. A set of nodes that can communicate with each other devoid of well-known infrastructure or centralized control is termed as multihop mobile ad hoc networks. Due to the transient nature of channel conditions, such a mechanism must be responsive to the changes with a small overhead. Traditional working protocols cannot work well in wireless ad-hoc network because of the characteristics of the wireless ad-hoc networks.[3]

Reference

[1]   G. Suseendran and A. Sasikumar, "Secure Intrusion-Detection System in Mobile Adhoc Networks," vol. 9, no. May, 2016.

[2]   A. Manet, "CHANNEL AWARE MAC PROTOCOL FOR MAXIMIZING THROUGHPUT AND FAIRNESS," vol. 3, no. 5, pp. 1–9, 2013.

[3]   G. Suseendran, E. Chandrasekaran, and A. R. Adaptation, "Channel Aware MAC Protocol with

5.3.   Citation Style

1. You can change the citation style of reference.

2. Click Reference Menu and you may find Style drop down list as shown in below screen.

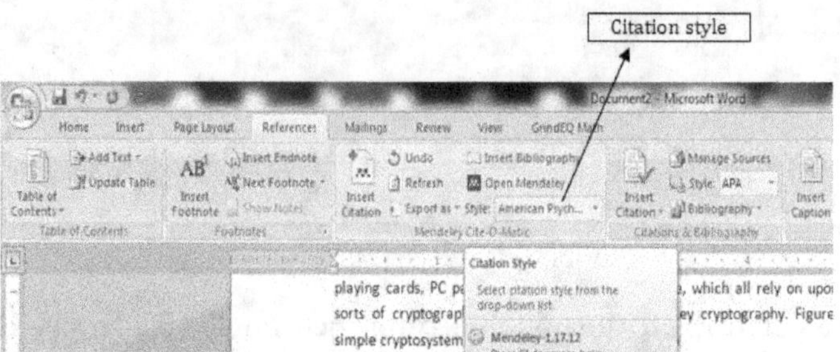

3. You may find the Citation style in the drop down list as below.

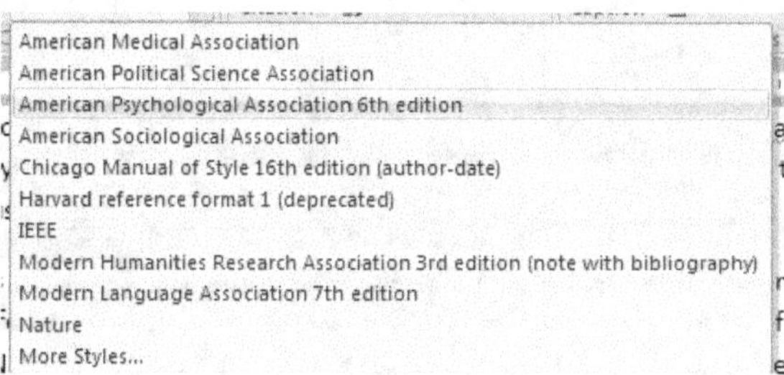

5.4.   American Medical Association

Wireless ad-hoc network is a set of wireless mobile nodes dynamically self organizing a temporary network without any central administration or existing network infrastructure. The node in the wireless ad-hoc network can provide as routers and hosts. Hence they can forward packets for other nodes if they are on route from source to destination. In wireless communications, rate adaptation is a mechanism for the sender to determine an appropriate data transfer rate to use the channel to the maximum extent. A set of nodes that can communicate with each other devoid of well-known infrastructure or centralized control is termed as multihop mobile ad hoc networks. Due to the transient nature of channel conditions, such a mechanism must be responsive to the changes with a small overhead. Traditional working protocols cannot work well in wireless ad-hoc network because of the characteristics of the wireless ad-hoc networks.[3] ← Reference No. Marked in Superscript and Author name arranged Last Name and First Name

Reference

1.   Suseendran G, Sasikumar A. Secure Intrusion-Detection System in Mobile Adhoc Networks. 2016;9(May). doi:10.17485/ijst/2016/v9i19/93829.

2.   Manet A. CHANNEL AWARE MAC PROTOCOL FOR MAXIMIZING THROUGHPUT AND FAIRNESS. 2013;3(5):1-9. doi:10.7815/ijorcs.

3.   Suseendran G, Chandrasekaran E, Adaptation AR. Channel Aware MAC Protocol with Rate Adaptation for MANET. 2013;2(1):13-18.

5.5.   American Political Science Association

Wireless ad-hoc network is a set of wireless mobile nodes dynamically self organizing a temporary network without any central administration or existing network infrastructure. The node in the wireless ad-hoc network can provide as routers and hosts. Hence they can forward packets for other nodes if they are on route from source to destination. In wireless communications, rate adaptation is a mechanism for the sender to determine an appropriate data transfer rate to use the channel to the maximum extent. A set of nodes that can communicate with each other devoid of well-known infrastructure or centralized control is termed as multihop mobile ad hoc networks. Due to the transient nature of channel conditions, such a mechanism must be responsive to the changes with a small overhead. Traditional working protocols cannot work well in wireless ad-hoc network because of the characteristics of the wireless ad-hoc networks.(Suseendran, Chandrasekaran, and Adaptation 2013)

Reference No. Marked by Author followed by year of publication

Reference

Manet, A. 2013. "CHANNEL AWARE MAC PROTOCOL FOR MAXIMIZING THROUGHPUT AND FAIRNESS." 3(5): 1–9.

Suseendran, G, E Chandrasekaran, and A Rate Adaptation. 2013. "Channel Aware MAC Protocol with Rate Adaptation for MANET." 2(1): 13–18.

Suseendran, G. and A Sasikumar. 2016. "Secure Intrusion-Detection System in Mobile Adhoc Networks." 9(May).

5.6.   American Psychological Association 6th Edition

References

Author Name and Year of Publication

1. A. Manet, "Channel Aware Mac Protocol for Maximizing Throughput and Fairness", Vol. 3, No. 5, Pp. 1–9, 2013. https://doi.org/10.7815/ijorcs.

2. G. Suseendran, E. Chandrasekaran and A.R. Adaptation, "Channel Aware MAC Protocol with Rate Adaptation for MANET", Vol. 2, No. 1, Pp. 13–18, 2013.

3. G. Suseendran and A. Sasikumar, "Secure Intrusion-Detection System in Mobile Adhoc Networks", 2016. https://doi.org/10.17485/ijst/2016/v9i19/93829

Chapter–VI

6.1. Inserting Citation using Source Manager

1. Open MS–Word and delete all the reference and cited in paragraph.

2. It displays the screen as below.

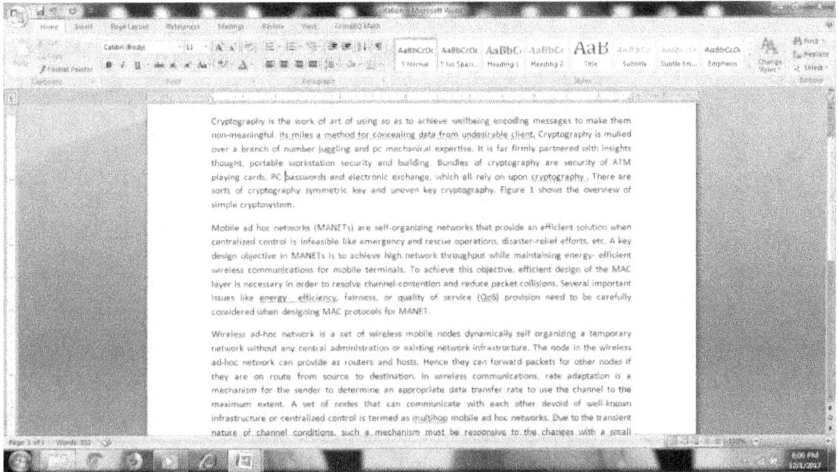

3. Click Reference Menu and you may see the Mendeley Tool Bar with Manage Source icon.

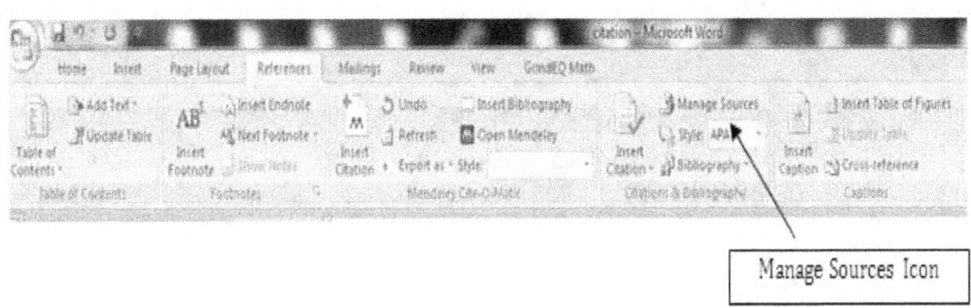

4. Click Manage Source Icon on the Tool Bar.

5. It display a screen as below.

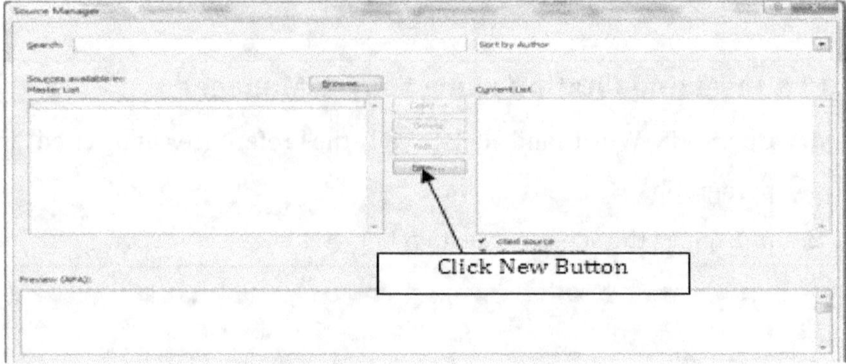

6. Click New Button on the screen as shown below.

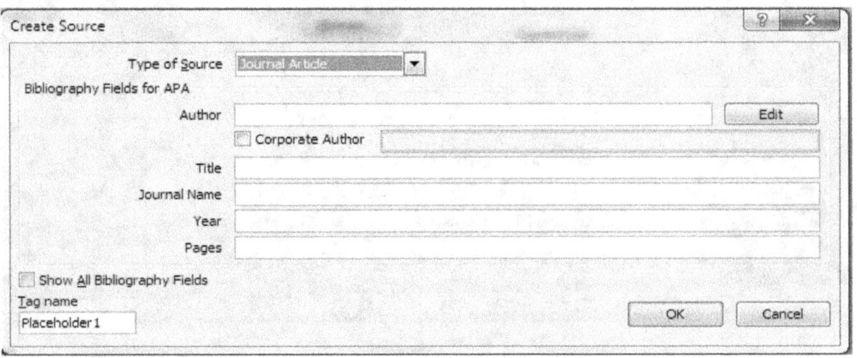

7. Click the Type of Source from the drop down list to select type of source for your citation. It displays a list.

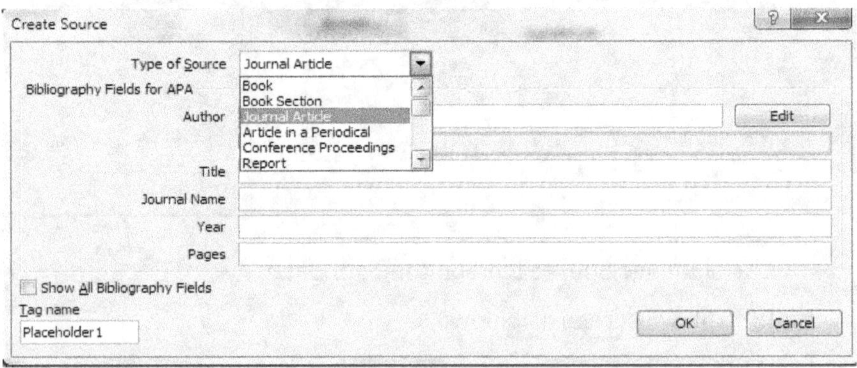

8. Select Type of Source as **Journal Type** and enter the following fields of source of article you want to include in citation.

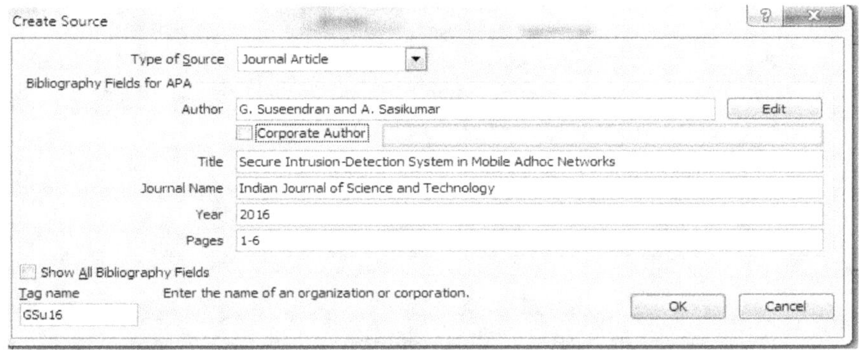

9. Click Ok Button to add in the Source List as displayed below.

10. You may notice the citation of the paper is added in the Source Manager.

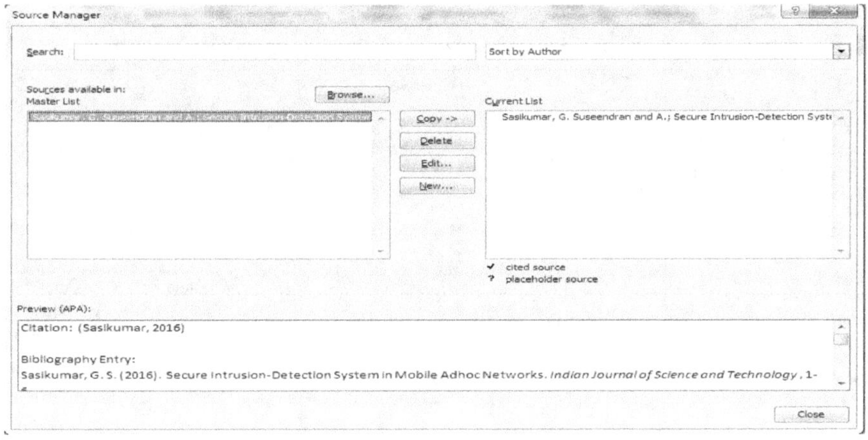

11. Click New Button from the Source Manager to include another citation in the source manager.

12. Enter the Details as mentioned below of second article you want to include in Ms-Word.

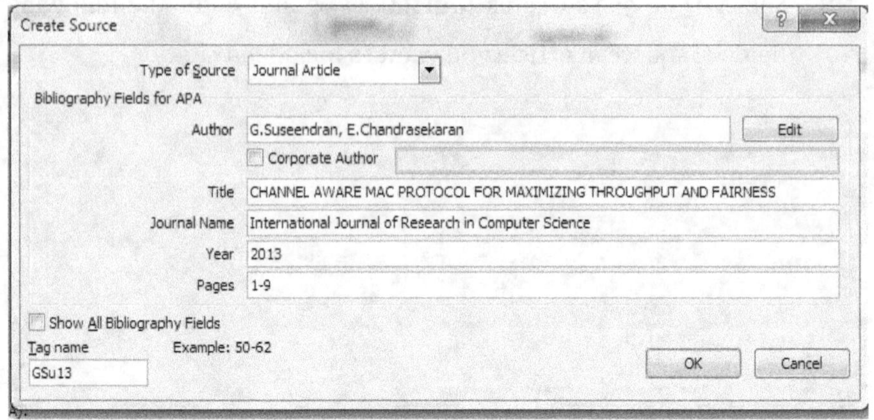

13. After enter the details Click ok Button to add the details of reference in the source manager.

14. It displays the second reference in the Source Manager as below screen.

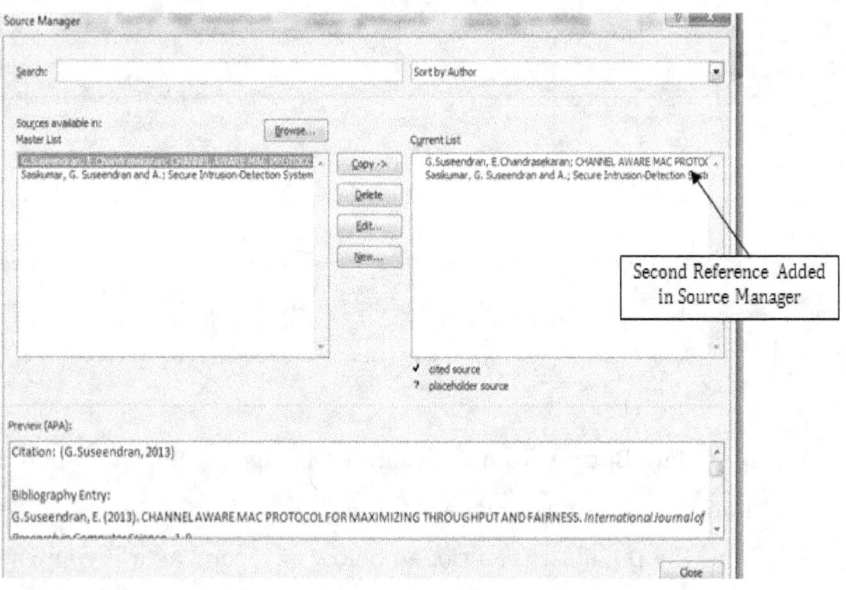

15. Now Click New Button to Add another reference in the Source Manager as listed below.

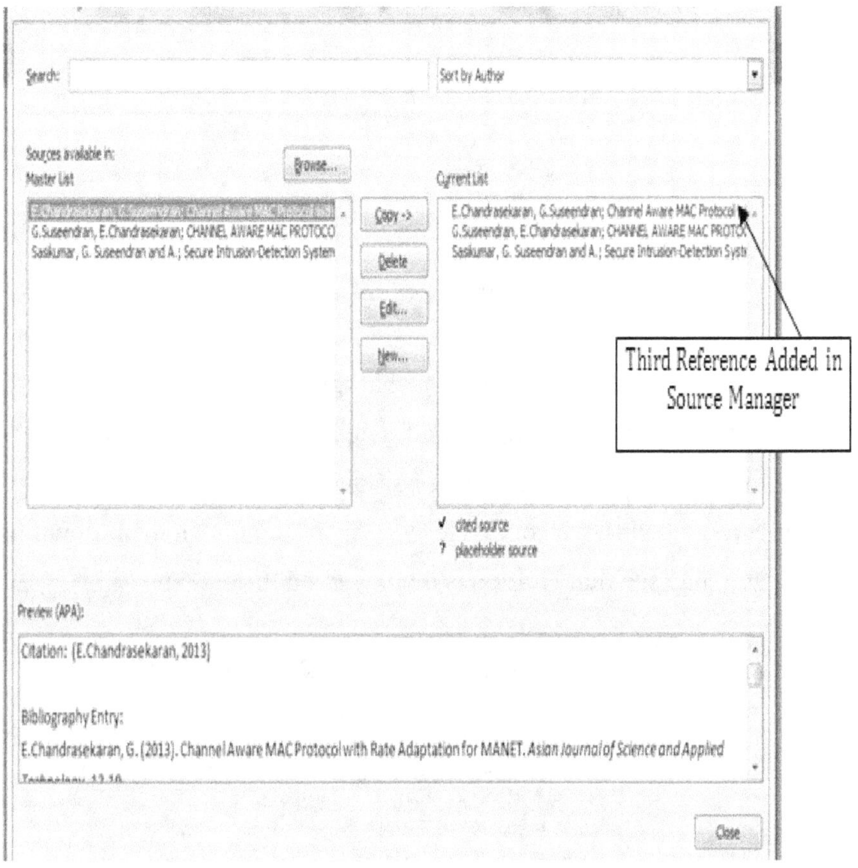

16. After Adding the Reference in the Source Manager Click Close Button.

17. Now Click Reference Menu and Click drop down arrow in Insert Citation Icon as displayed below.

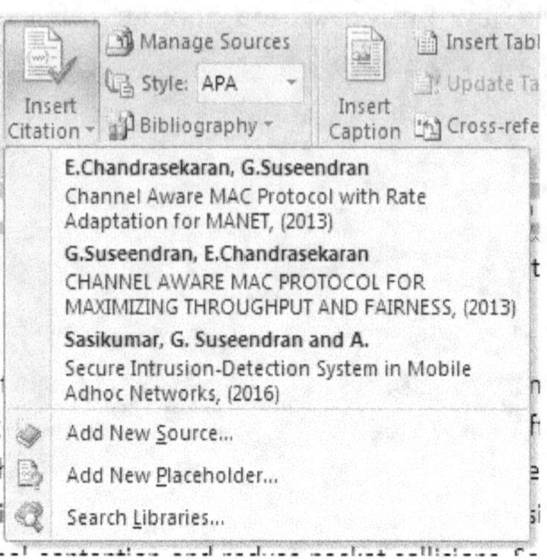

18. Now place the cursor on the paragraph you want to mark the citation of the document and select the reference you want to make the citation of selected paragraph as below.

19. Now I click the Second reference from the above drop down list you may see that citation is displayed on the screen.

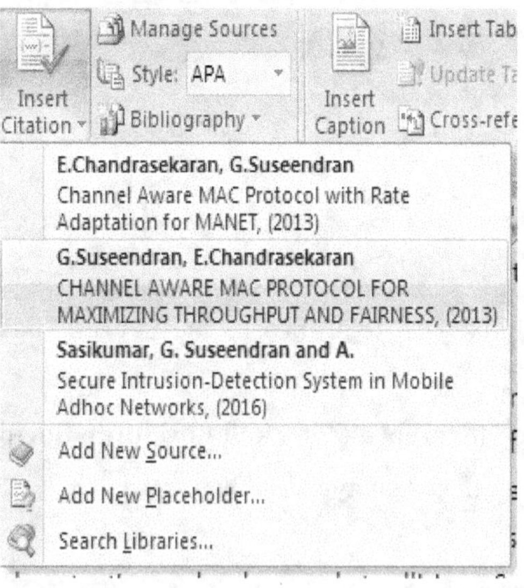

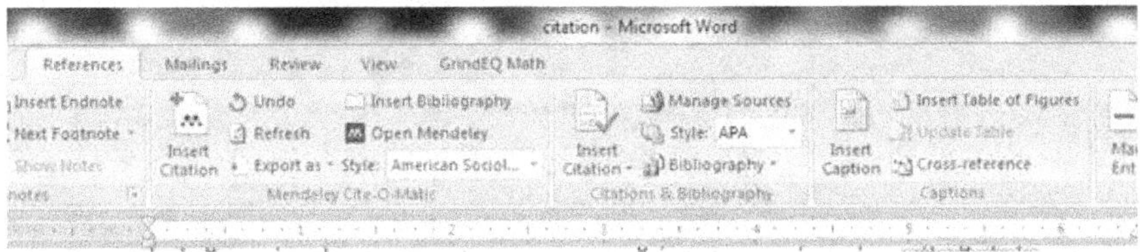

sorts of cryptography symmetric key and uneven key cryptography. Figure 1 shows the overview of simple cryptosystem.

Mobile ad hoc networks (MANETs) are self-organizing networks that provide an efficient solution when centralized control is infeasible like emergency and rescue operations, disaster-relief efforts, etc. A key design objective in MANETs is to achieve high network throughput while maintaining energy- efficient wireless communications for mobile terminals. To achieve this objective, efficient design of the MAC layer is necessary in order to resolve channel-contention and reduce packet collisions. Several important issues like energy efficiency, fairness, or quality of service (QoS) provision need to be carefully considered when designing MAC protocols for MANET.

Wireless ad-hoc network is a set of wireless mobile nodes dynamically self organizing a temporary network without any central administration or existing network infrastructure. The node in the wireless ad-hoc network can provide as routers and hosts. Hence they can forward packets for other nodes if they are on route from source to destination. In wireless communications, rate adaptation is a mechanism for the sender to determine an appropriate data transfer rate to use the channel to the maximum extent. A set of nodes that can communicate with each other devoid of well-known infrastructure or centralized control is termed as multihop mobile ad hoc networks. Due to the transient nature of channel conditions, such a mechanism must be responsive to the changes with a small overhead. Traditional working protocols cannot work well in wireless ad-hoc network because of the characteristics of the wireless ad-hoc networks. (G.Suseendran, 2013) ⟶ Citation Inserted

20. Now Place the cursor on the next paragraph you want to mark the citation.

21. Click Insert Citation and select the second reference you want to cite as displayed below.

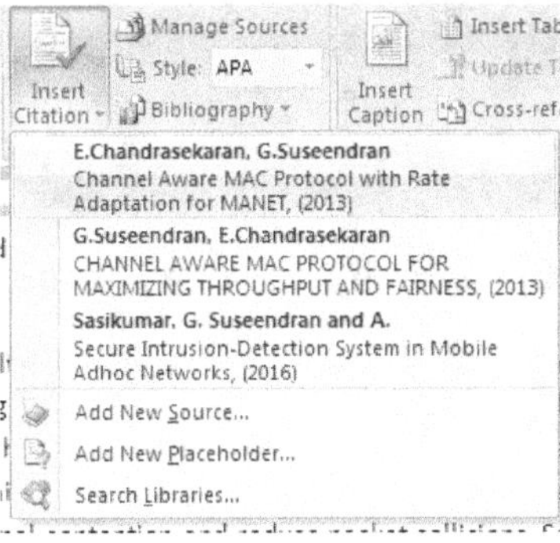

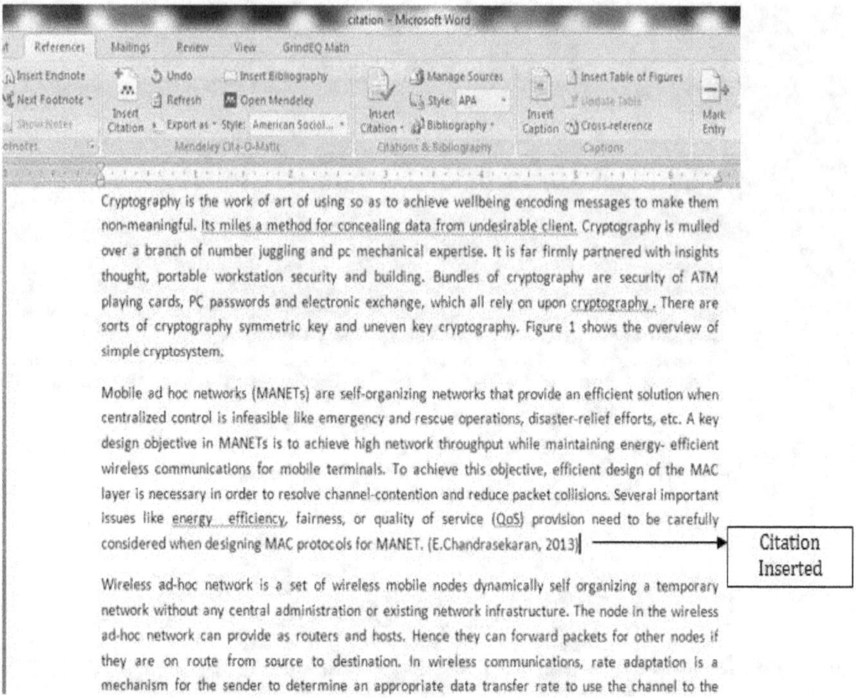

22. After adding all citation Click Bibliography icon from the Tool Bar as below.

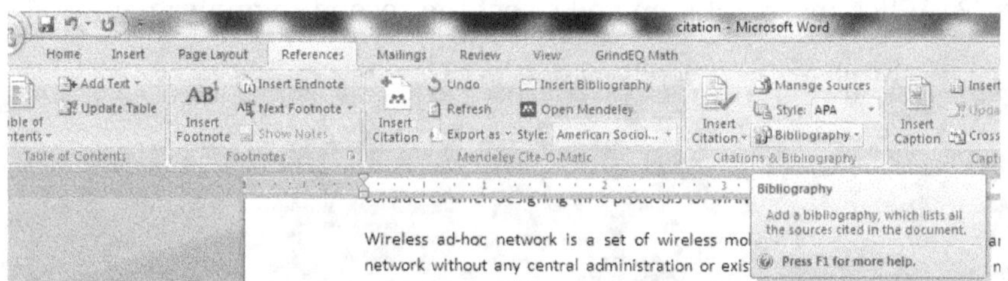

23. It display a Bibliography style you want to insert select the Bibliography style as listed below and click to add the Bibliography.

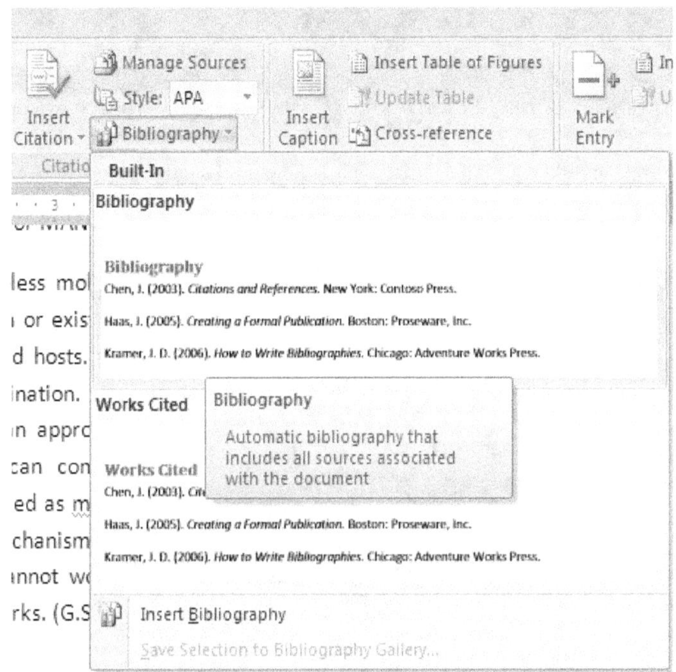

24. Click on the Bibliography style you may notice the Bibliography add in the document.

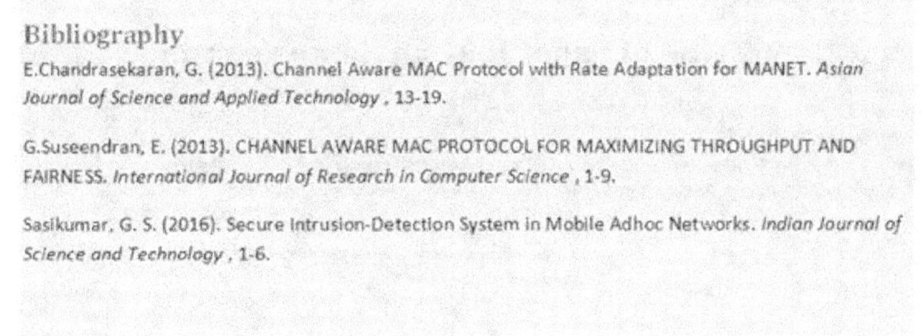

6.2. Source Citation Style

1. Click the Reference Menu and you may find the Style Drop Down list as shown below.

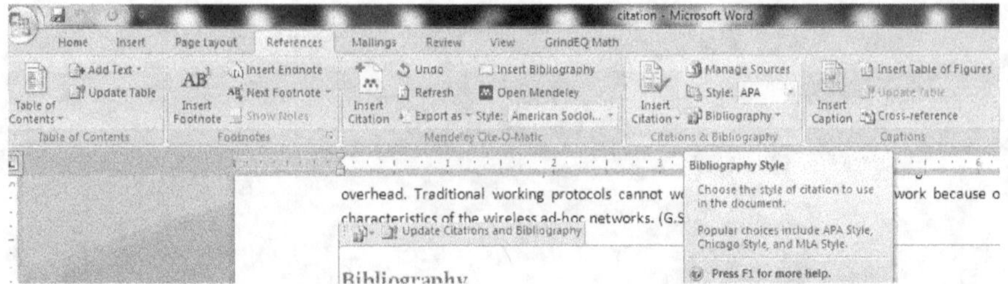

2. Click the drop down list to select the style of Bibliography you
    need.

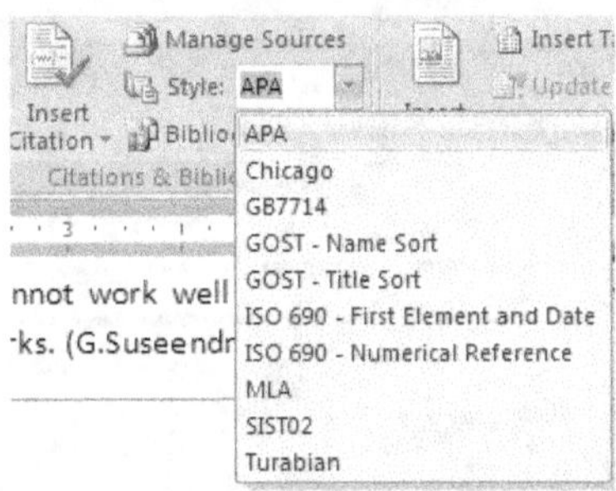

3. From the Style list select **Chicago** style you may notice the style
    change in Bibiligraphy.

    Chicago Style

Author Name Title of Paper Journal Name Year and Page No.

Bibliography

E.Chandrasekaran, G.Suseendran. "Channel Aware MAC Protocol with Rate Adaptation for MANET." *Asian Journal of Science and Applied Technology*, 2013: 13-19.

G.Suseendran, E.Chandrasekaran. "CHANNEL AWARE MAC PROTOCOL FOR MAXIMIZING THROUGHPUT AND FAIRNESS." *International Journal of Research in Computer Science*, 2013: 1-9.

Sasikumar, G. Suseendran and A. "Secure Intrusion-Detection System in Mobile Adhoc Networks." *Indian Journal of Science and Technology*, 2016: 1-6.

4. Now Select APA Style you may notice the Bibliography Style.

Author Name Second Author only Initial Year of Publication Title of Paper Journal Name and Page No.

He

⟨illegible garbled text⟩ networks. (G.Suseendran, 2013)
🔄 ▾ ✎ Update Citations and Bibliography

Bibliography

E.Chandrasekaran, G. (2013). Channel Aware MAC Protocol with Rate Adaptation for MANET. *Asian Journal of Science and Applied Technology* , 13-19.

G.Suseendran, E. (2013). CHANNEL AWARE MAC PROTOCOL FOR MAXIMIZING THROUGHPUT AND FAIRNESS. *International Journal of Research in Computer Science* , 1-9.

Sasikumar, G. S. (2016). Secure Intrusion-Detection System in Mobile Adhoc Networks. *Indian Journal of Science and Technology* , 1-6.

5. Now Select the Style **GB7714** may notice the Bibliography Style changes as given below.

   Title of the Paper Author Name Year Year Journal Name and Page No.

Bibliography

CHANNEL AWARE MAC PROTOCOL FOR MAXIMIZING THROUGHPUT AND FAIRNESS. **G.Suseendran, E.Chandrasekaran. 2013.** 2013, International Journal of Research in Computer Science, pp. 1-9.

Channel Aware MAC Protocol with Rate Adaptation for MANET. **E.Chandrasekaran, G.Suseendran. 2013.** 2013, Asian Journal of Science and Applied Technology, pp. 13-19.

Secure Intrusion-Detection System in Mobile Adhoc Networks. **Sasikumar, G. Suseendran and A. 2016.** 2016, Indian Journal of Science and Technology, pp. 1-6.

6. Now Select the Style GOST Name Sort may notice the Bibliography Style changes as given below.

Bibliography

E.Chandrasekaran G.Suseendran Channel Aware MAC Protocol with Rate Adaptation for MANET [Journal] // Asian Journal of Science and Applied Technology. - 2013. - pp. 13-19.

G.Suseendran E.Chandrasekaran CHANNEL AWARE MAC PROTOCOL FOR MAXIMIZING THROUGHPUT AND FAIRNESS [Journal] // International Journal of Research in Computer Science. - 2013. - pp. 1-9.

Sasikumar G. Suseendran and A. Secure Intrusion-Detection System in Mobile Adhoc Networks [Journal] // Indian Journal of Science and Technology. - 2016. - pp. 1-6.

7. Now select the GOST Title Sort may notice the Bibliography Style changes as given below.

Bibliography

CHANNEL AWARE MAC PROTOCOL FOR MAXIMIZING THROUGHPUT AND FAIRNESS [Journal] / auth.
G.Suseendran E.Chandrasekaran // International Journal of Research in Computer Science. - 2013. - pp.
1-9.

Channel Aware MAC Protocol with Rate Adaptation for MANET [Journal] / auth. E.Chandrasekaran
G.Suseendran // Asian Journal of Science and Applied Technology. - 2013. - pp. 13-19.

Secure Intrusion-Detection System in Mobile Adhoc Networks [Journal] / auth. Sasikumar G.
Suseendran and A. // Indian Journal of Science and Technology. - 2016. - pp. 1-6.

8. Now select the **MLA** may notice the Bibliography Style changes as given below.

Bibliography

E.Chandrasekaran, G.Suseendran. "Channel Aware MAC Protocol with Rate Adaptation for MANET."
Asian Journal of Science and Applied Technology (2013): 13-19.

G.Suseendran, E.Chandrasekaran. "CHANNEL AWARE MAC PROTOCOL FOR MAXIMIZING THROUGHPUT
AND FAIRNESS." International Journal of Research in Computer Science (2013): 1-9.

Sasikumar, G. Suseendran and A. "Secure Intrusion-Detection System in Mobile Adhoc Networks." Indian
Journal of Science and Technology (2016): 1-6.

9. Now select the **ISO 690 - Numerical Reference** may notice the Bibliography Style changes as given below.

Bibliography

1. *Secure Intrusion-Detection System in Mobile Adhoc Networks.* **Sasikumar, G. Suseendran and A.** 2016,
Indian Journal of Science and Technology, pp. 1-6.

2. *Channel Aware MAC Protocol with Rate Adaptation for MANET.* **E.Chandrasekaran, G.Suseendran.**
2013, Asian Journal of Science and Applied Technology, pp. 13-19.

3. *CHANNEL AWARE MAC PROTOCOL FOR MAXIMIZING THROUGHPUT AND FAIRNESS.* **G.Suseendran,
E.Chandrasekaran.** 2013, International Journal of Research in Computer Science, pp. 1-9.

Chapter–VII

7.1.   Creating Group

1. Open Mendeley Software.

2. Click New Group on Left Hand Side of the screen or Click Edit Menu Choose New Group option.

3. It display a screen as below.

4. Click Private to Share your PDF article to your friends to prepare for Research Papers.

5. Click Create Button to create a group on Private Access.

6. It displays a Message to Create the Group Name on the Same screen as shown below.

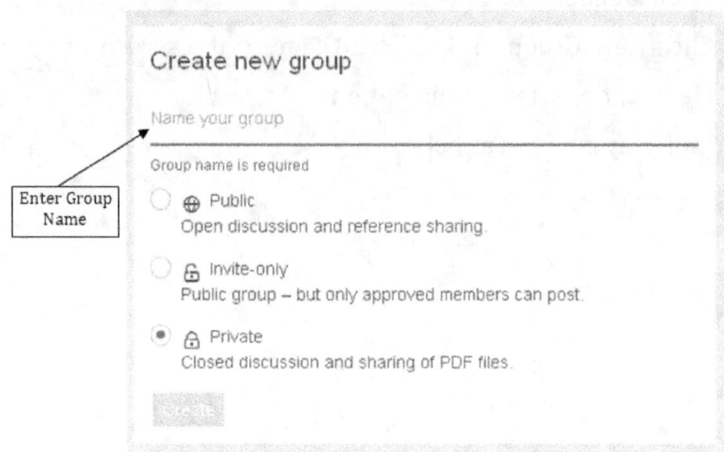

7. Now enter the group name as "Suseendar-MANET".

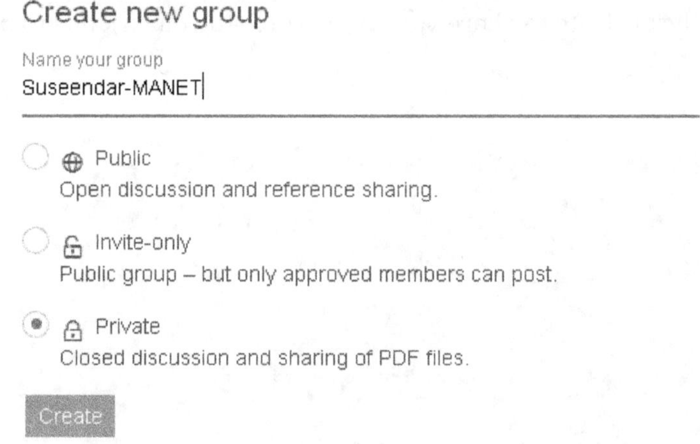

8. You may notice that the group name is created on the left side of the window as shown below.

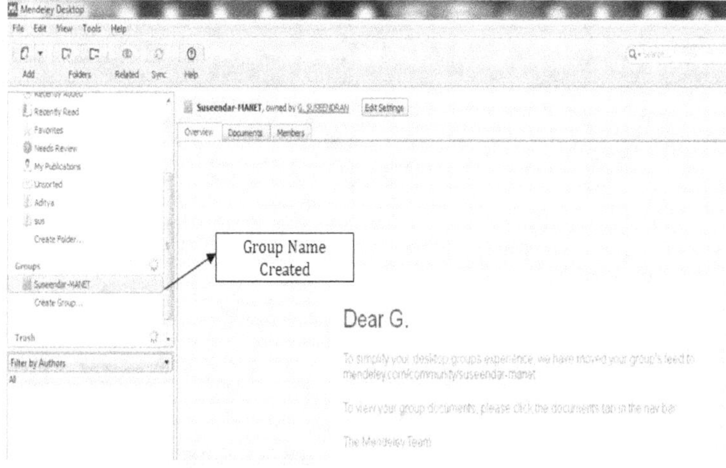

9. Click the Link to go to Mendeley Group It display a Login Screen.

10. Enter your Mendeley Login and Password and Click Login.

11. It display a browser of your group as shown below.

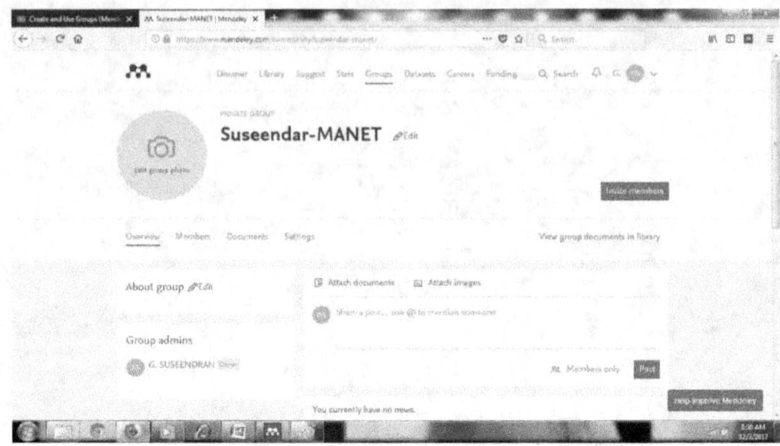

12. Click Edit Photo to load your Photo of your group It display a screen.

13. Click Upload Image it display a screen to upload the photo of your group as displayed below.

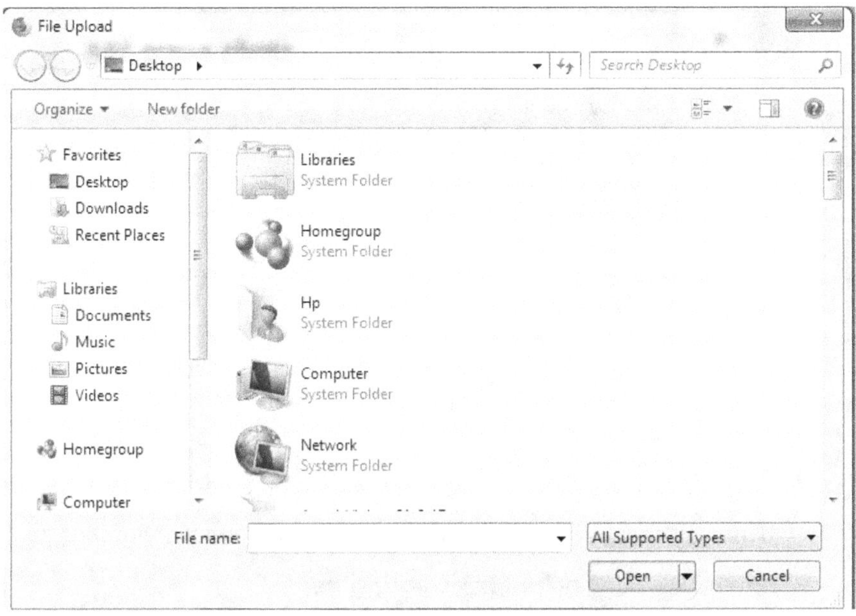

14. Select your drive in which your photo to upload in the group.

15. Select the Photo and press **Set the group Picture** Button as displayed below.

16. You may notice that Group Picture is loaded as displayed in the screen.

17. To logout from the Group Click GS Icon on Right Side of the Browser click on the icon it display a drop down is from that drop down list you may find Log Out Option.

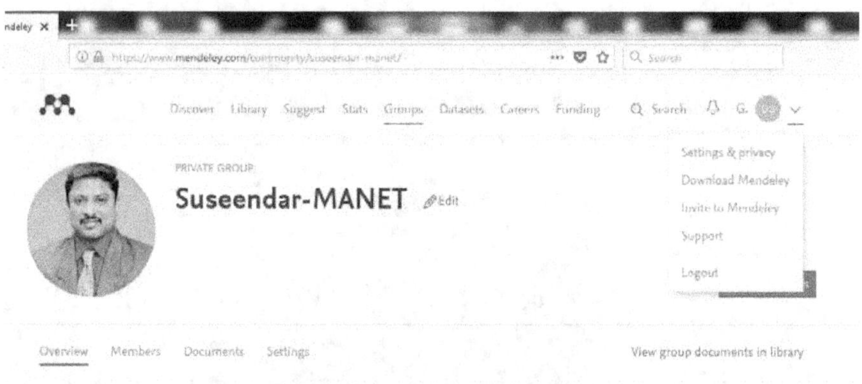

7.2.   Adding Document in Group Library

1. Type www.mendeley.com website.

2. It display a Login Page Enter the Login Name and Password to Login to Mendeley.

3. It display a screen as below.

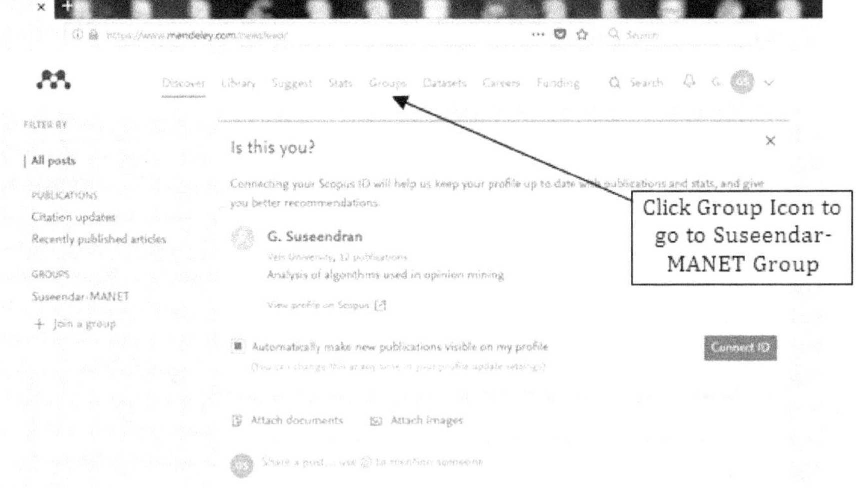

4. Click Group Menu to go to the Suseendar-MANET group as display below.

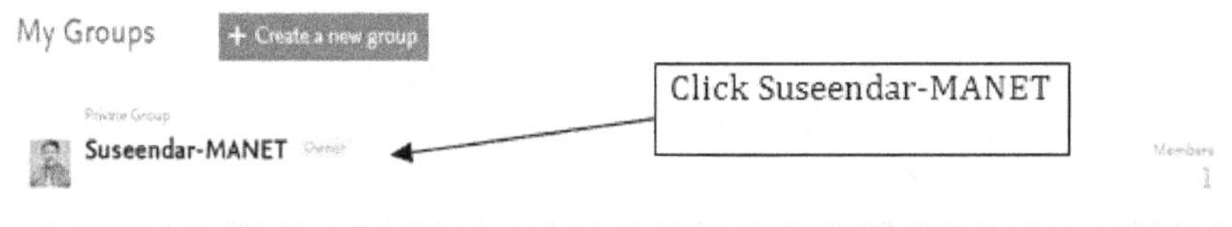

5. Click Suseendar-MANET group name to enter in to the group.
6. It display the screen as below.

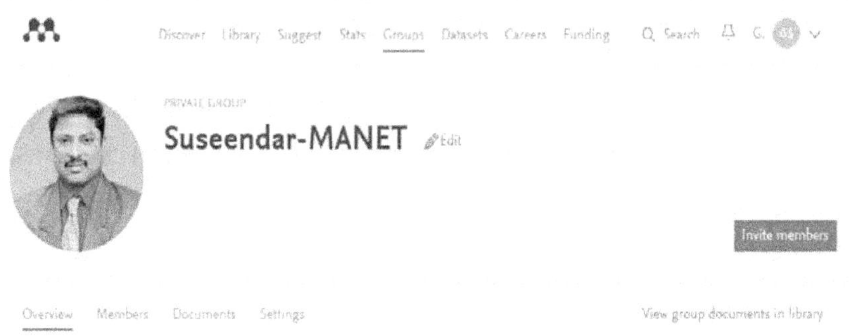

7. Click Documents Tab from the screen.

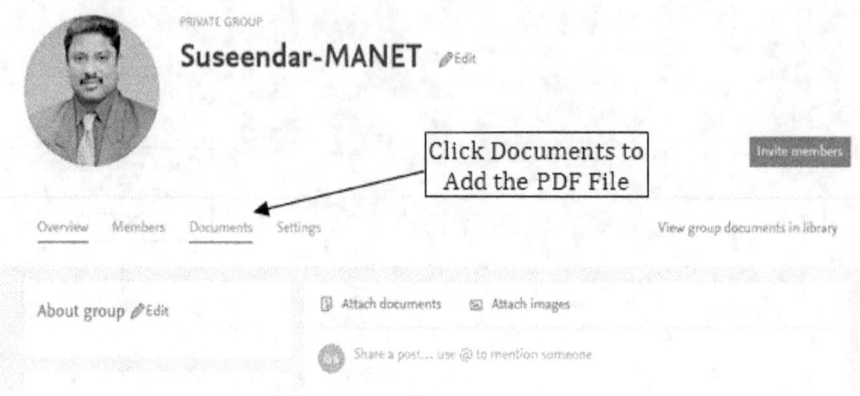

8. It display a screen as below.

Documents

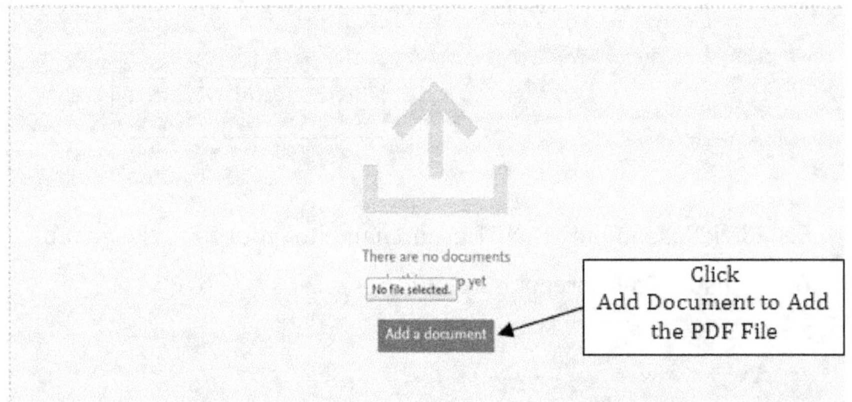

9. It display a screen to choose the PDF file to add in the Group.

10. Select the PDF document and click open button to add in the Group.

11. It display the screen as shown the Paper Title of the Paper as shown below.

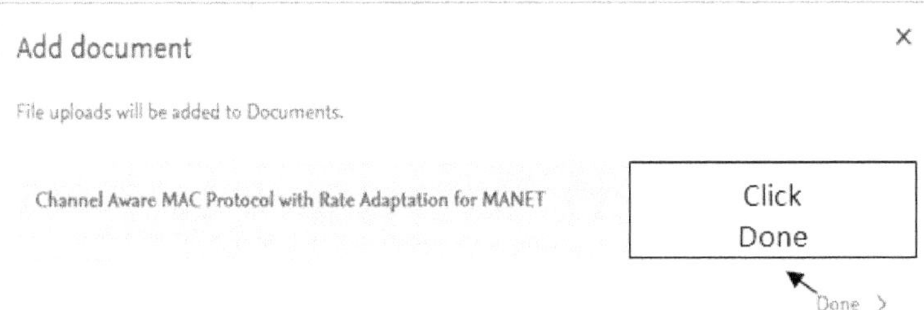

12. Click **Done** Tab to add the document in the Group.

13. You may see the paper is add in the group as shown below.

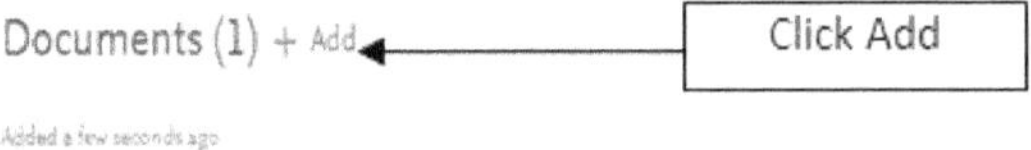

14. Click Add Tab to add another document in the Group.

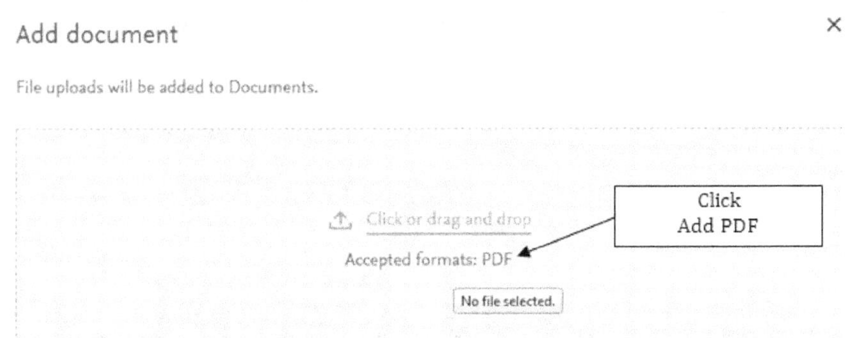

15. Click Accepted format PDF to add another document.

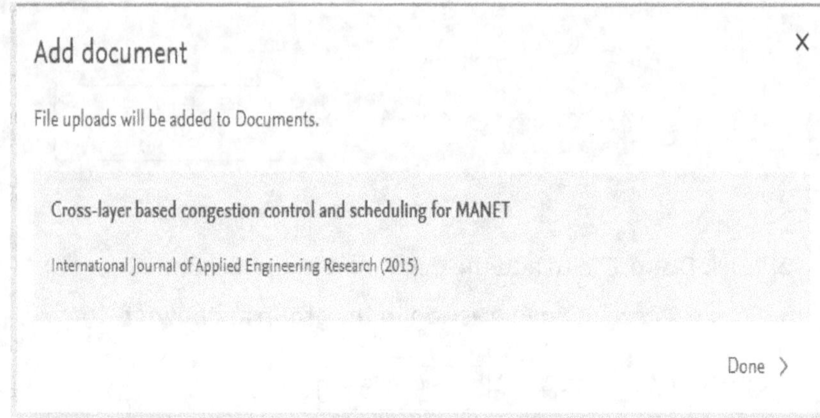

16. You may notice the list of document is added in the list.

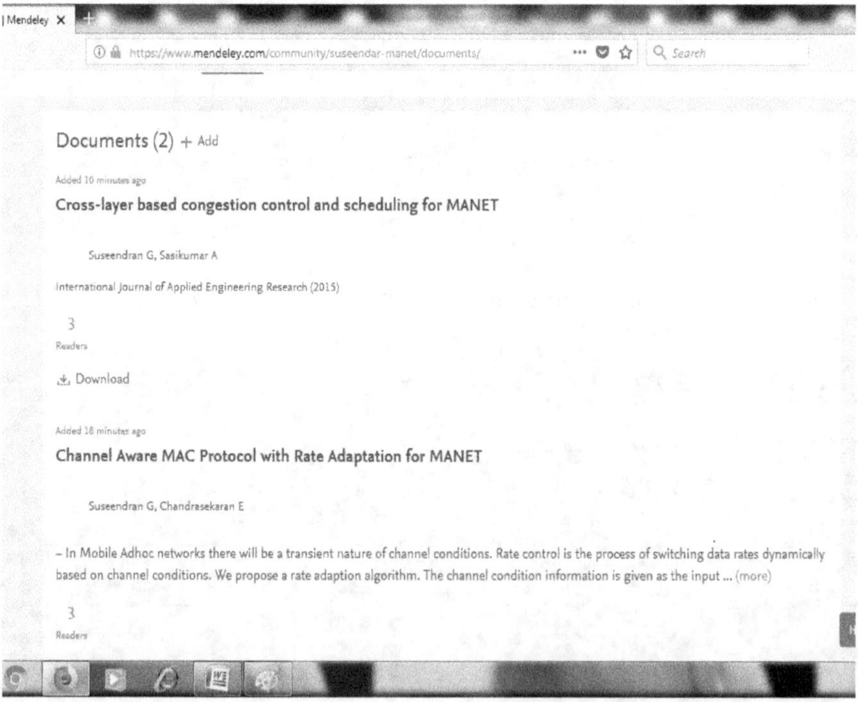

7.3.   View Group Document in Library

1.   Click View Group Document in Library Tab.

2.   It display a screen as below to view the document in Library.

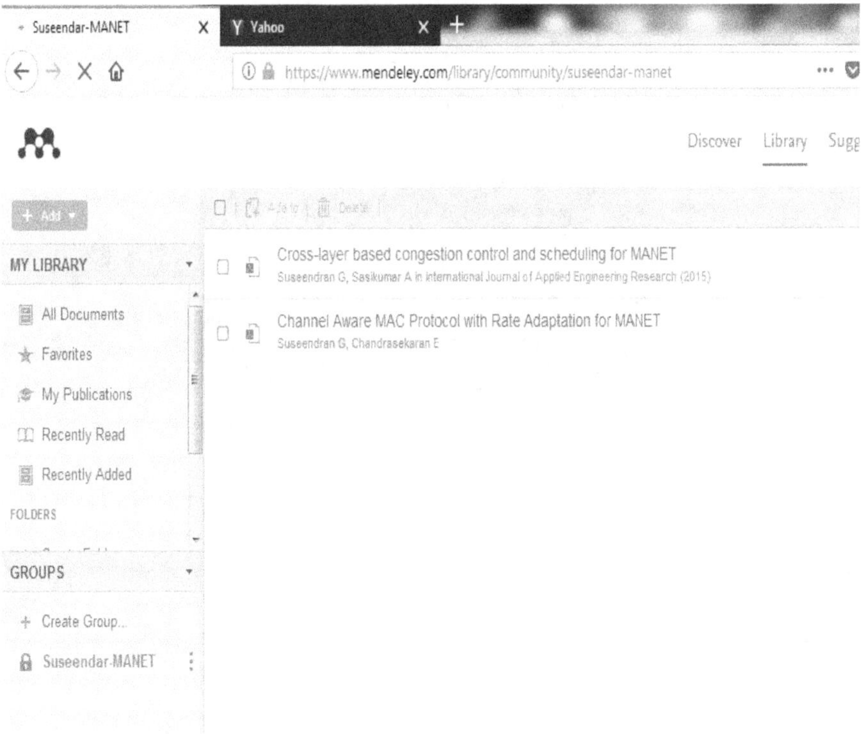

3. You may notice the list of document is added in the Library.

4. To Open the document in Mendeley Library Double Click the Title of the Paper.

5. The PDF Open as displayed below.

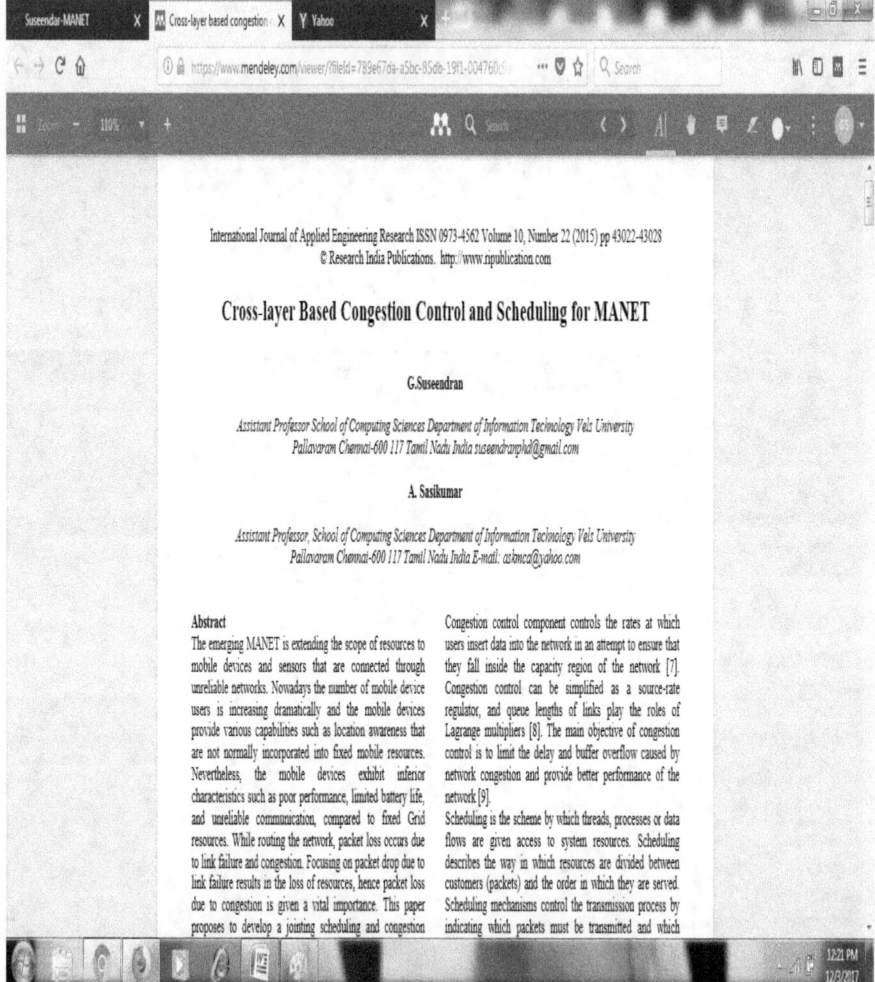

International Journal of Applied Engineering Research ISSN 0973-4562 Volume 10, Number 22 (2015) pp 43022-43028
© Research India Publications. http://www.ripublication.com

Cross-layer Based Congestion Control and Scheduling for MANET

G.Suseendran

Assistant Professor School of Computing Sciences Department of Information Technology Vels University Pallavaram Chennai-600 117 Tamil Nadu India suseendranphd@gmail.com

A. Sasikumar

Assistant Professor, School of Computing Sciences Department of Information Technology Vels University Pallavaram Chennai-600 117 Tamil Nadu India E-mail: asknca@yahoo.com

Abstract

The emerging MANET is extending the scope of resources to mobile devices and sensors that are connected through unreliable networks. Nowadays the number of mobile device users is increasing dramatically and the mobile devices provide various capabilities such as location awareness that are not normally incorporated into fixed mobile resources. Nevertheless, the mobile devices exhibit inferior characteristics such as poor performance, limited battery life, and unreliable communication, compared to fixed Grid resources. While routing the network, packet loss occurs due to link failure and congestion. Focusing on packet drop due to link failure results in the loss of resources, hence packet loss due to congestion is given a vital importance. This paper proposes to develop a jointing scheduling and congestion

Congestion control component controls the rates at which users insert data into the network in an attempt to ensure that they fall inside the capacity region of the network [7]. Congestion control can be simplified as a source-rate regulator, and queue lengths of links play the roles of Lagrange multipliers [8]. The main objective of congestion control is to limit the delay and buffer overflow caused by network congestion and provide better performance of the network [9].

Scheduling is the scheme by which threads, processes or data flows are given access to system resources. Scheduling describes the way in which resources are divided between customers (packets) and the order in which they are served. Scheduling mechanisms control the transmission process by indicating which packets must be transmitted and which

6. To close the PDF Click Close Tab on the title bar to close the PDF Document.

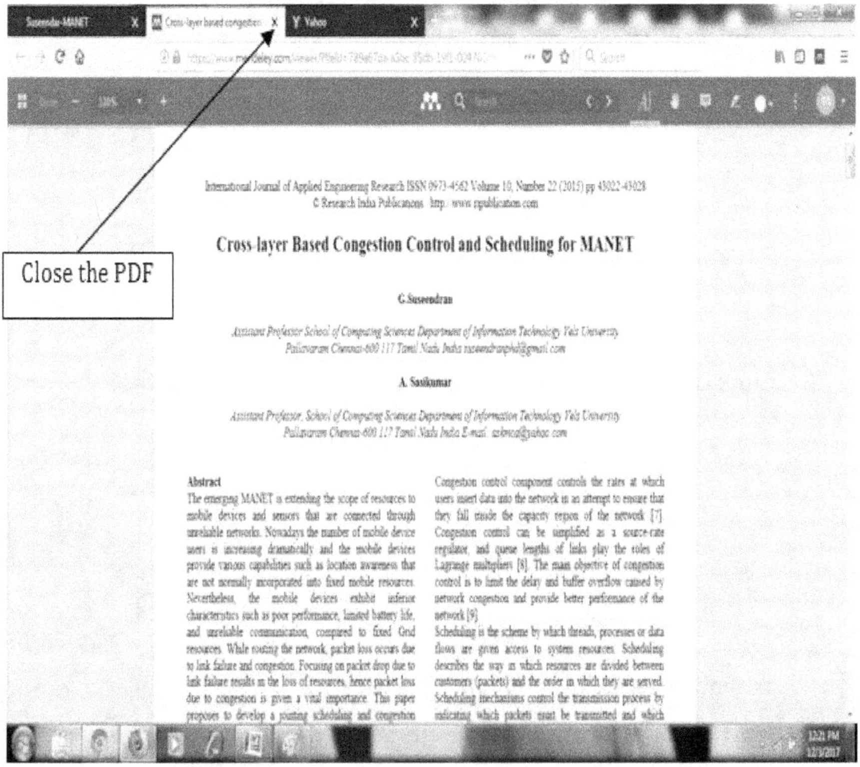

7.4. Deleting Files in Library

1. Click the Check Box on the List of Document Library.

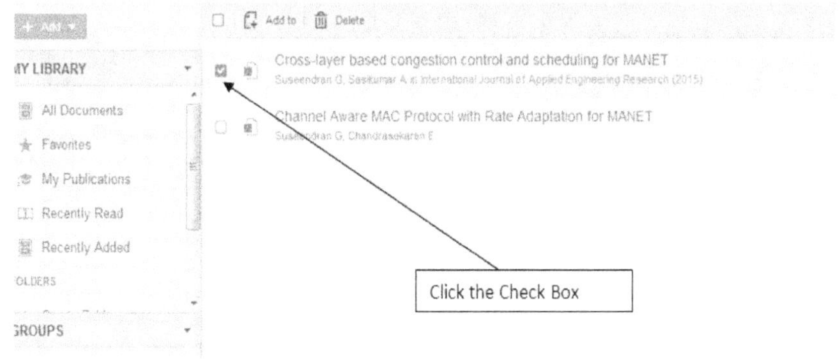

2. Click Delete Tab on the Screen to Delete the PDF.

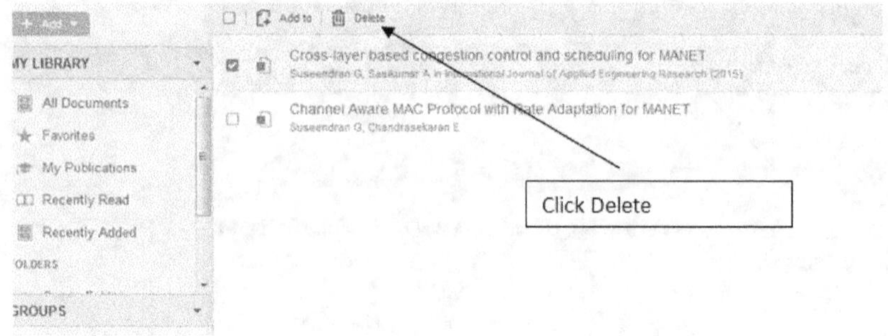

3. Click Delete Tab to Delete the PDF from the Library.

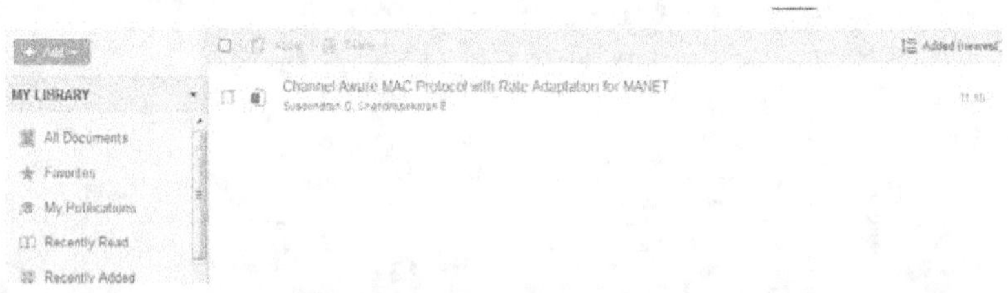

4. You may notice one Document is deleted from the Library.

5. Now Delete Another Document from the Library now may screen that no document is inserted in the Library.

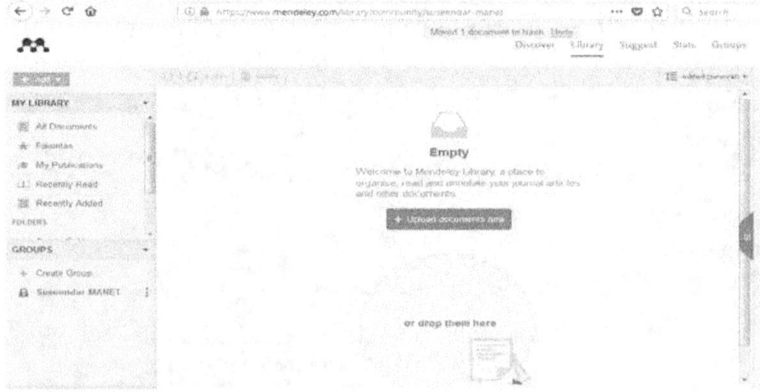

6. Now Logout from the Group.

7.5. Adding Documents in Mendeley Library using Drag and Drop

1. Open Mendeley Software.

2. Select the PDF and drag the PDF to the Group Suseendar-MANET.

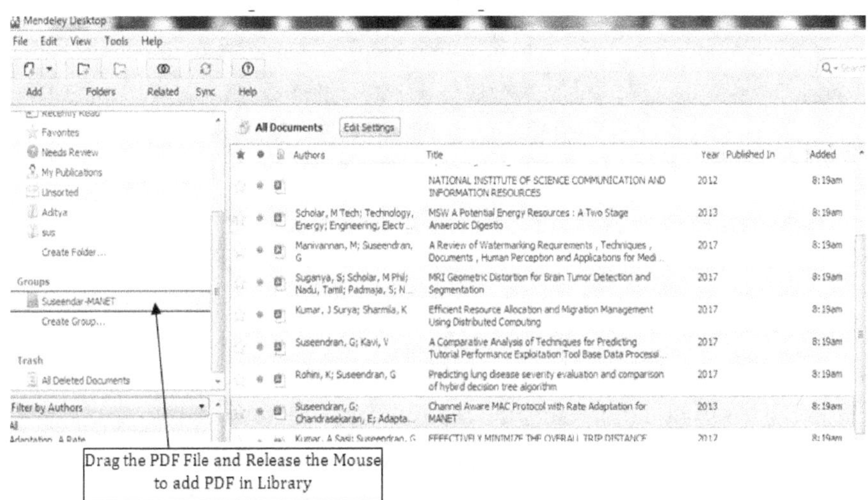

3. If you want to add two or more file at time Press Ctrl+Click the document and move to the Group Suseendar-MANET.

4. Now Click the Group Suseendar-MANET as the screen display.

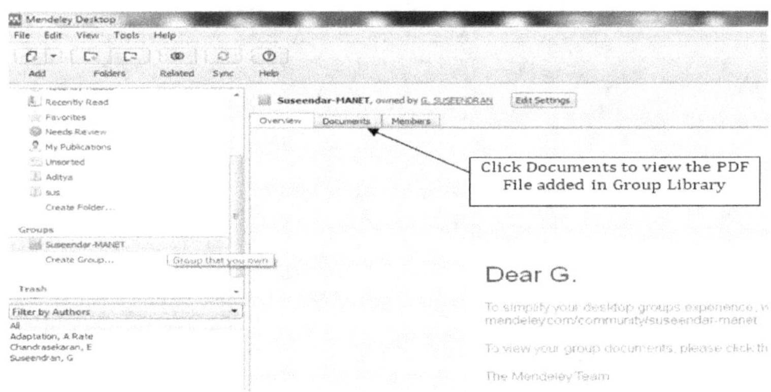

5. Now click the Documents Tab on the Screen to view the PDF document added in the Library.

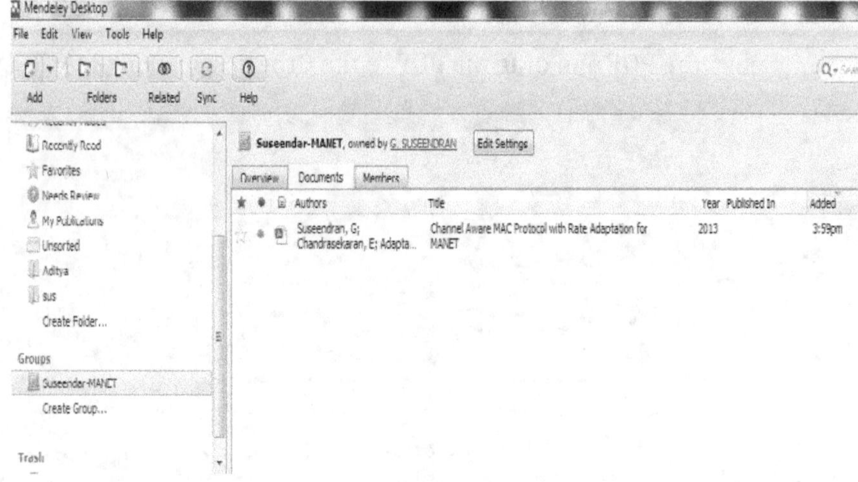

6. Now Click File Menu and Sign out from Mendeley.

7. Open the web browser type www.mendeley.com

8. Click Sign In and Enter the Email Address and password to login to group.

9. Now Click Groups the screen display.

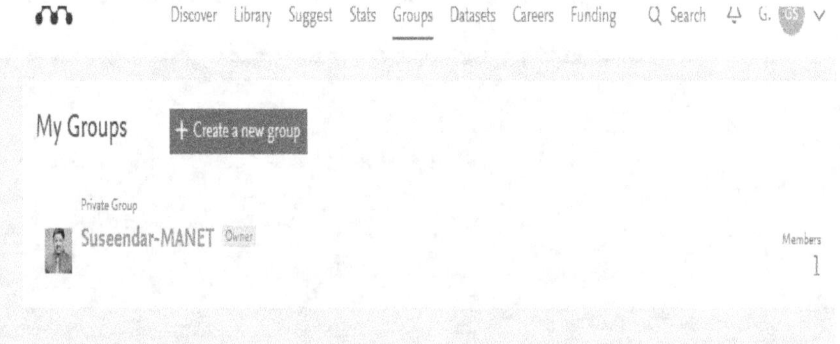

10. You may notice the PDF article is loaded.

11. Click View Group Document in Library It display a Library.

12. You may notice that the Document is added in the Library as shown in the screen.

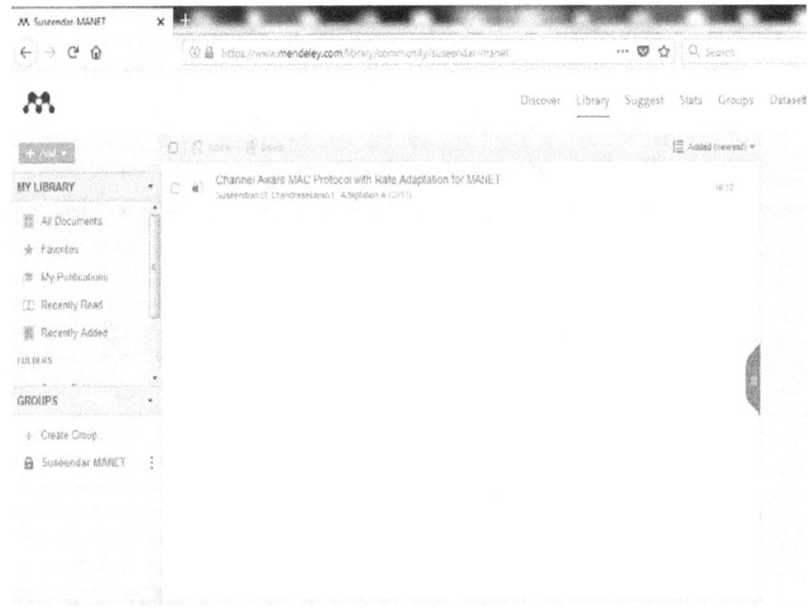

7.6.   Inviting Your Friend to Group

1. Inform them to create a group and ask then to search your profile

2. Tel them to invite.

3. After Inviting Open the web browser.

4. Type www.mendeley.com You may find a name which is invited in your group as displayed in the screen.

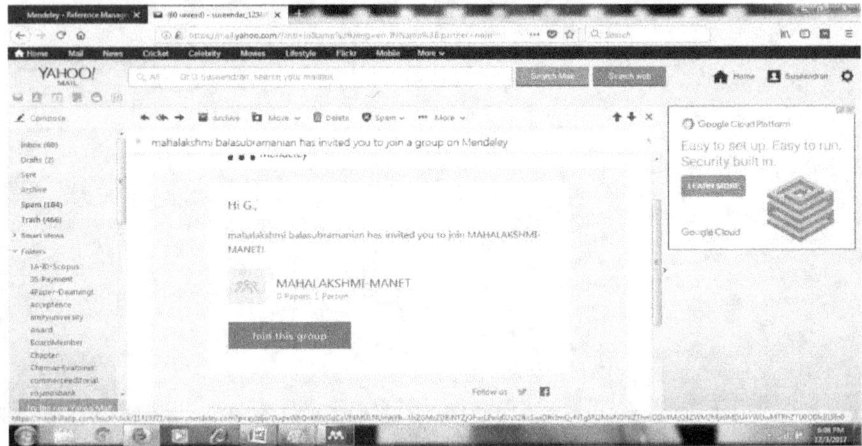

5. Login to your Email ID.

6. You have received a mail from Mendeley that your friend has accepted in your group as shown in the below screen.

7. Click Join this Group to join your friend to Suseendar-MANET group.

8. You may find that your friend has added in your group as displayed in the below screen.

7.7.   Creating Group Pubic

1. Open the Mendeley Software.

2. Click Create Group it display screen.

3. It display a screen.

4. Now Click Public it ask for Group name Enter the Group name as Suseendar-Cloud.

5. It display a screen to Sign in to Mendeley as shown below.

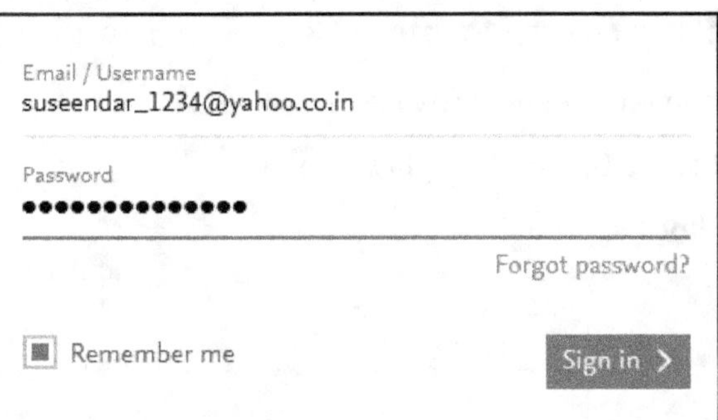

6. Enter the Email Address and Password to Sign in to Mendeley.

7. You may notice the group Suseendar-Cloud is created.

8. Click Back from the web browser to go to Home Page.

9. Click Discover Tab and you may find your friend and others on who want to include in your group on public access of your document.

10. You may notice the people will be displayed as shown below.

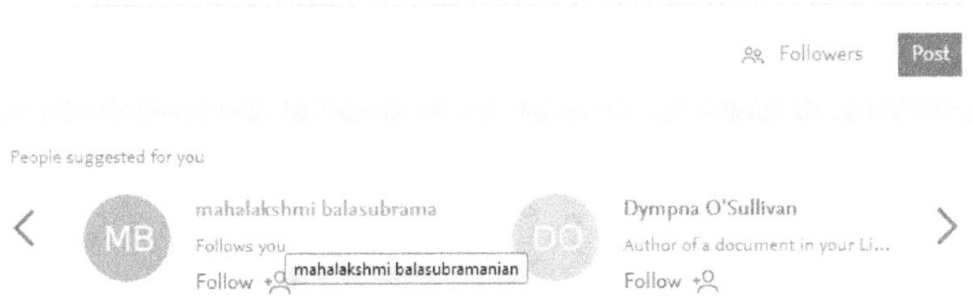

11. Click Mahalakhmi Balasubrama to go the group.

12. It display a screen.

13. Click Follow to follow the people in your group.

CHAPTER-VIII

8.1.   Web Importer

1. Go to Google Type as "Jelly Fish in MANET".

2. Click Search it displays as Search page on the related topic searched as below.

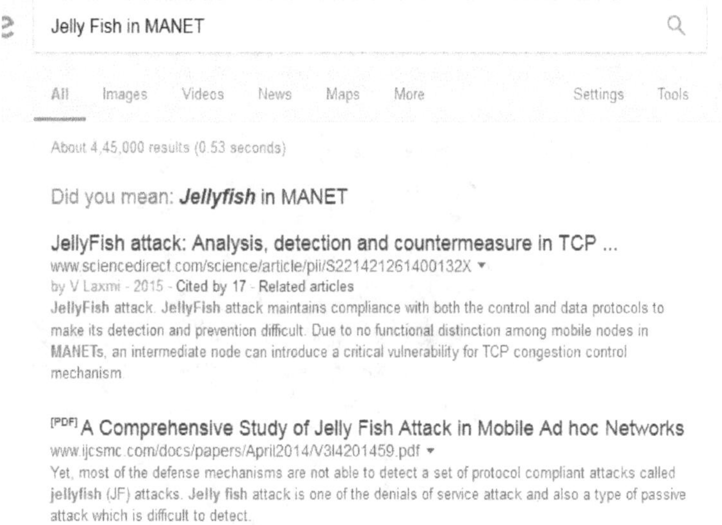

3. Click the title of the Search "A Comprehensive Study of Jelly Fish Attack in Mobile Ad hoc Network".

4. It displays a PDF File as displayed below.

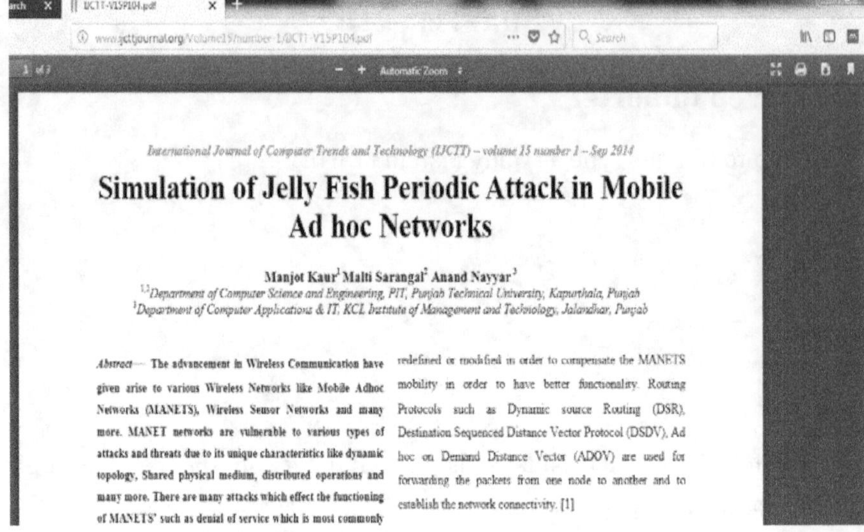

5. Click the Web Importer Icon on the web browser.

6. It displays a screen as below.

7. Click Sign in Button to Login to Mendeley.

8. It display a screen as below.

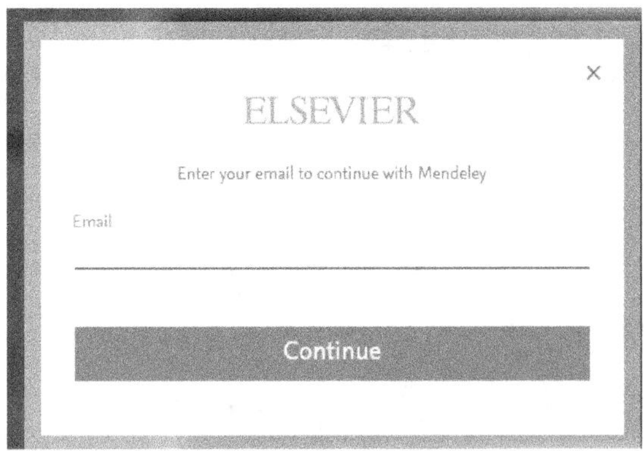

9. Enter the Email address and click continue.

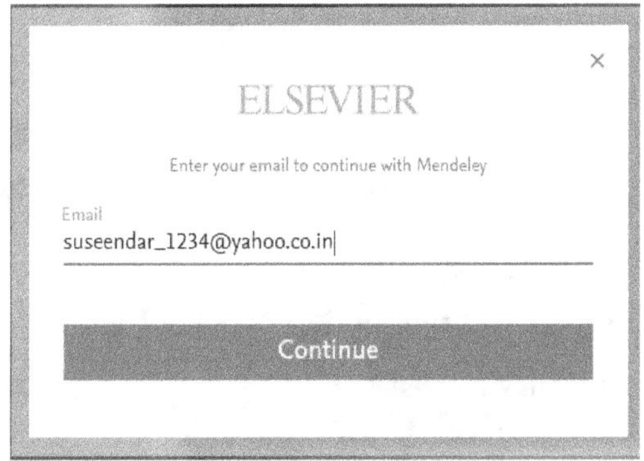

10. Enter the password and click continue button.

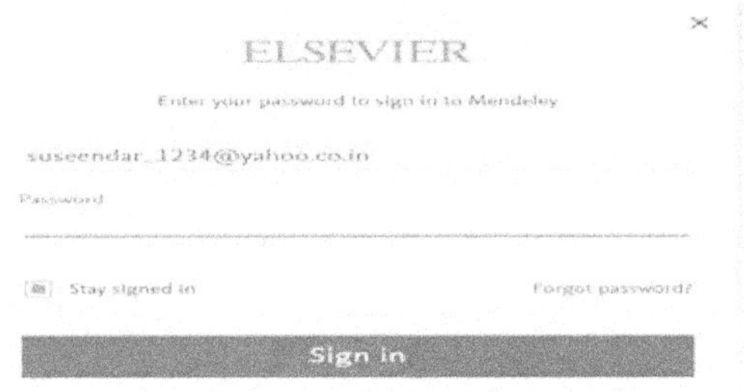

11. Now you may notice Mendeley open the details of the Contents of the PDF you viewed in the web browser as displayed below.

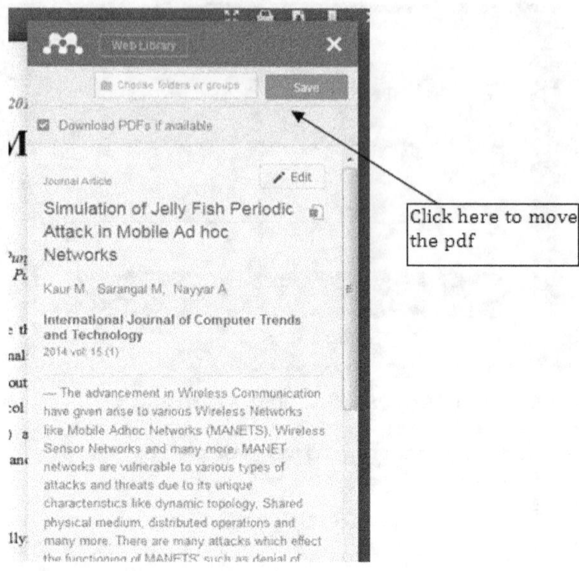

12. Now Click "Choose Folder of Groups" to move the file to Mendeley Library.

13. Click the Folder "Aditya" and Click Save Button to add the PDF to Mendeley Library.

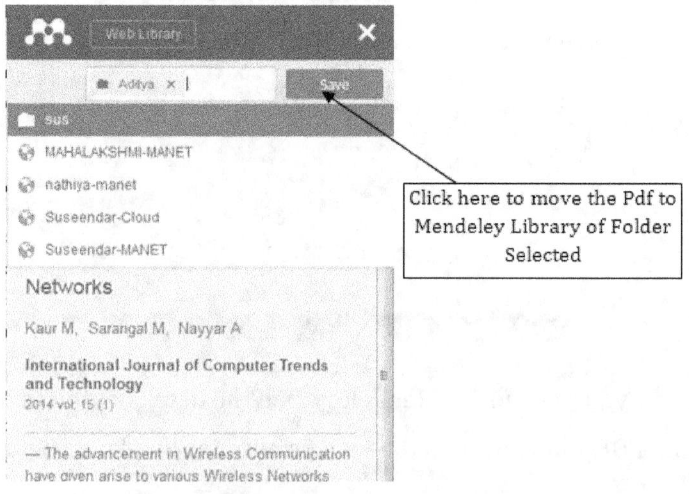

14. After clicking save Button Close the Web browser.

15. Open Mendeley Software and click **Aditya** Folder in the Mendeley Library.

16. You may notice the file is not added as given below.

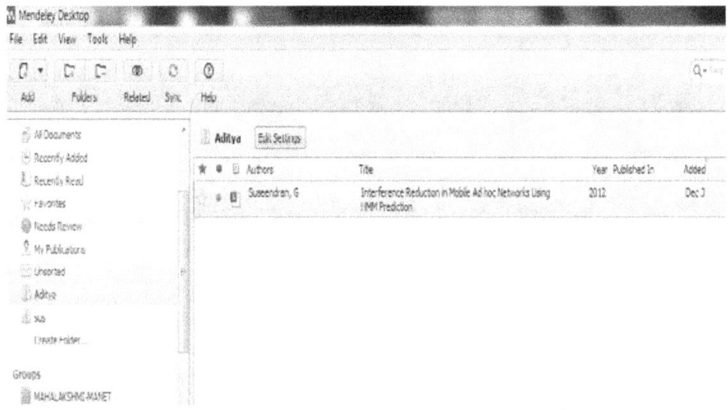

17. Click Sync Button to refresher the folder from cloud and you may notice the PDF file is added in the Folder of **Aditya.**

18. You may notice that the file uploaded in the Mendeley Library after clicking Sync Button on the Button.

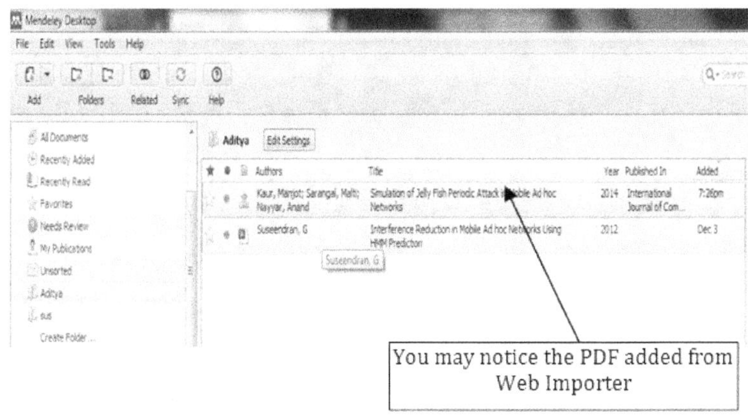

CHAPTER-IX

9.1.   Scopus Registration

1. In your browser type www.scopus.com.

2. It display a Scopus website as below screen shows.

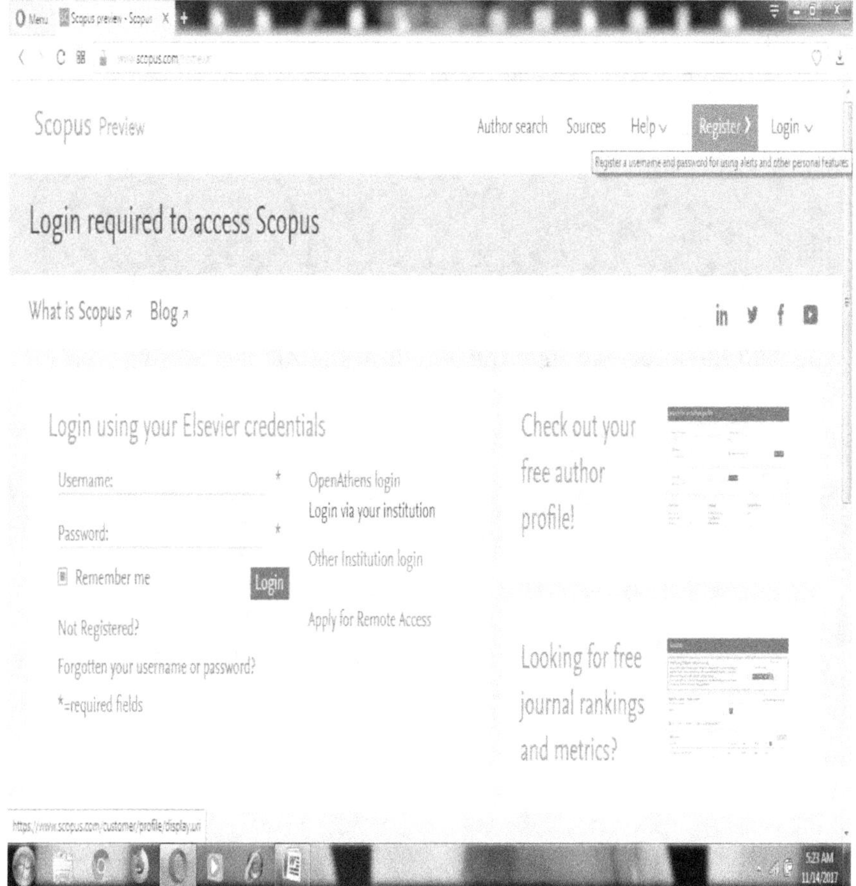

3. Click Register Button.

4. It display a Registration Screen as below.

Register

Registration is quick and free. It allows you to personalize the Elsevier products to which you have access.

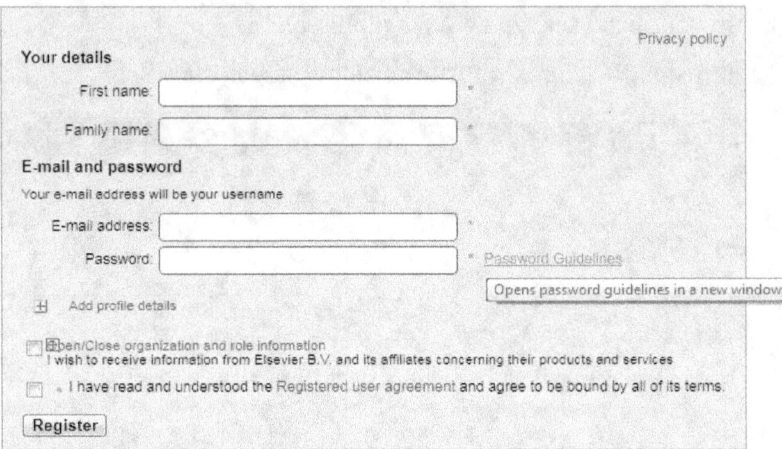

5.   Fill the information in the details as mentioned below.

Note: Use Email password don't change to new password.

6. After Typing the information Click Add Profile Details and enter the information.

Your job title

Job title: Assistant Professor

Your address

Phone number: 9840523133 (including country / region code)

Mailing address: New:59 Old:22/3, PA Koil Lane,

Ayanavaram, Chennai

City: Chennai

Postal (zip) code: 600023 (Required for Canada / US users)

Country / Region: India

State / province: Tamilnadu (Required for Canada / US users)

Open/Close organization and role information
I wish to receive information from Elsevier B.V. and its affiliates concerning their products and services

* I have read and understood the Registered user agreement and agree to be bound by all of its terms.

Register

7. After Typing the Information Click Open/Close Organization and Role Information To add your College name/ University Name

8. Enter your College Name in Organization Name

9. Now Click Your Role List Box and Select as Professor/ Associate or Faculty or Phd Student

   Click Faculty

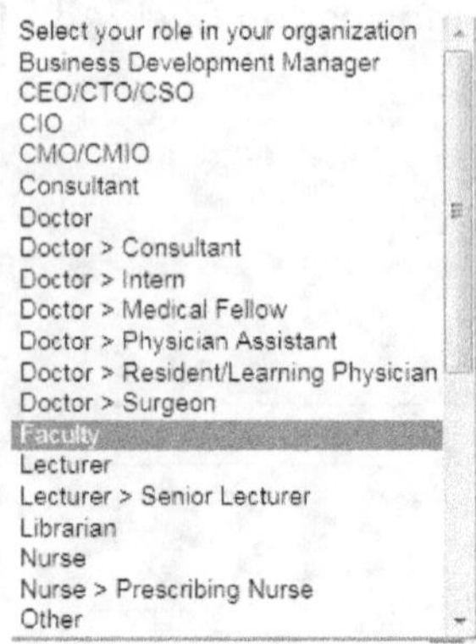

10. After Selecting Faculty from the role now select your Department as listed in Check box.

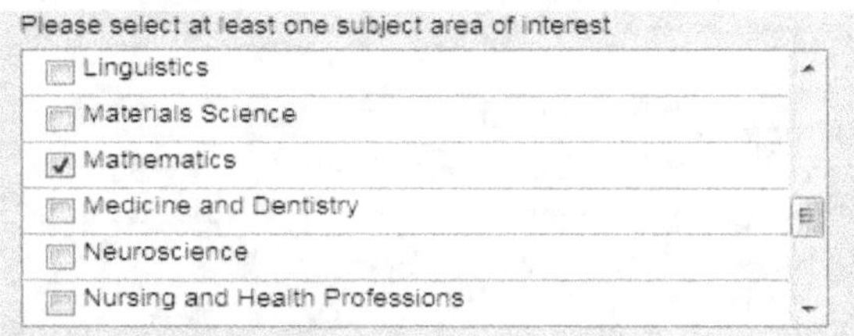

11. After Selecting the Department Click I have Read understood the Register and Click Register Button.

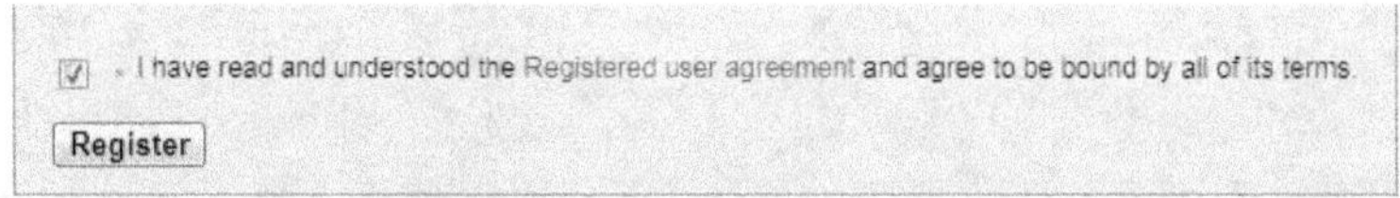

12. After Clicking Register Button Close the Internet Browser

13. Go to your email id and check u have received your mail from Scopus after Successful Registration.

9.2.   Searching Author Profile in Scopus

1. Go to the website www.scopus.com.

2. Displays a Scopus Web page.

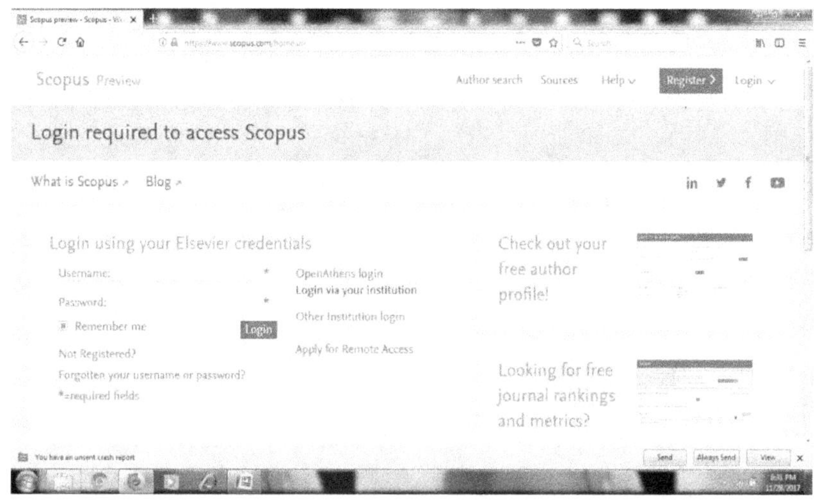

3. Click Author Search on the Top of the Screen

4. It Display as Screen as below

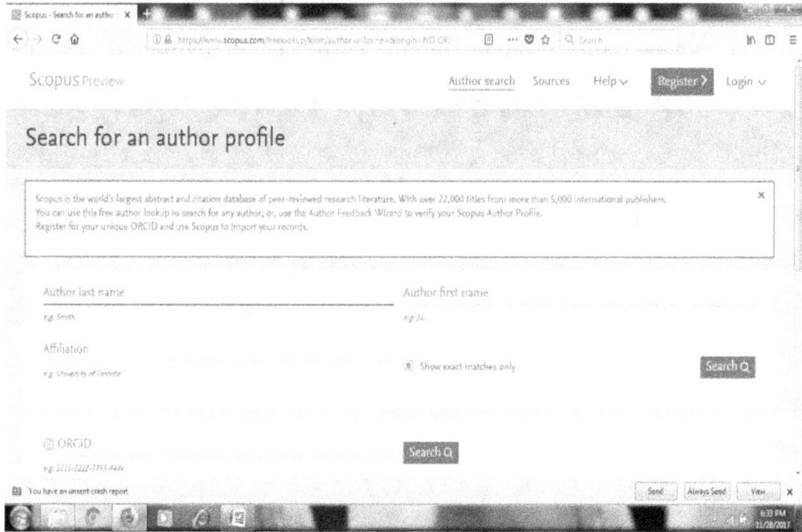

5. Click on Author Last Name to place the cursor to type the author name.

6. Enter the author name Suseendran and Author First Name as G.

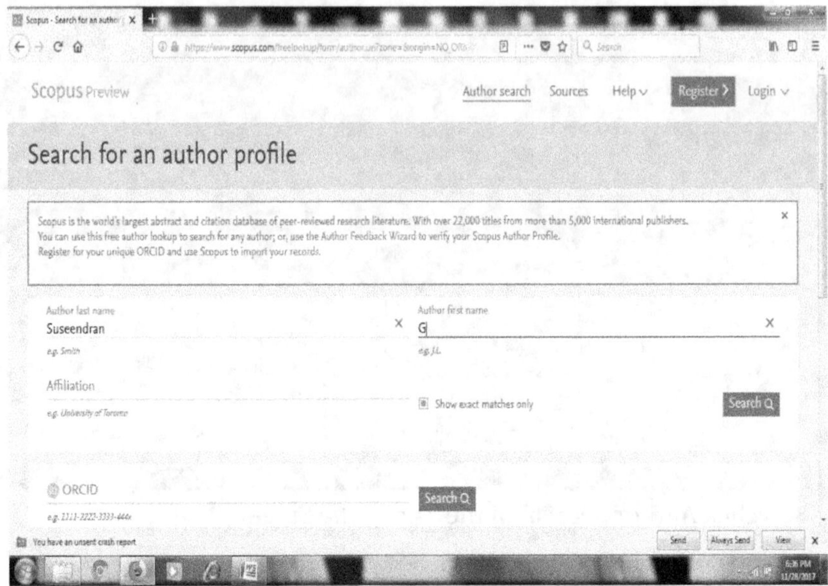

7.   Click Search Button to Search the author Profile.

8.   It displays the search of the above author as displayed below.

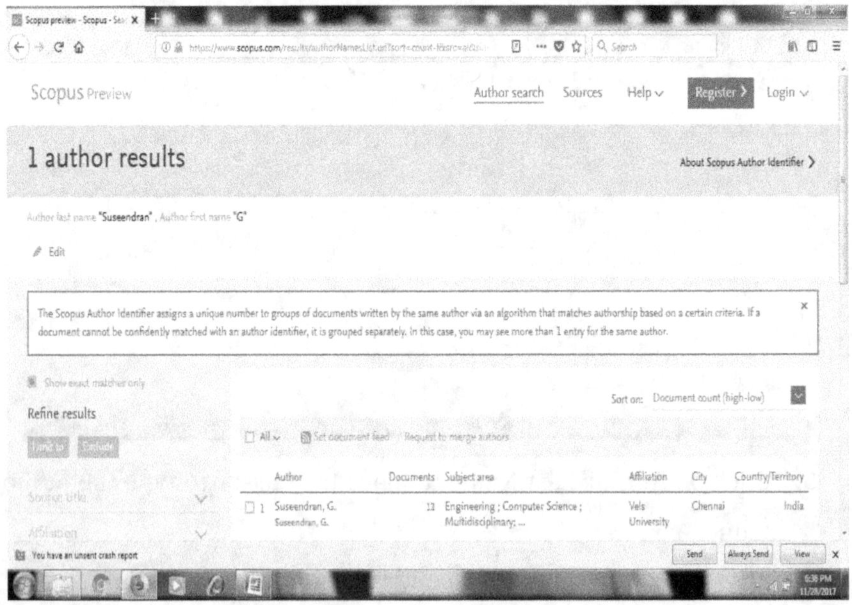

9. You can find name of the author and number of article indexed in the Scopus Database.

10. Now Click the Author name to view the list of Publication.

9.3. Searching Journal indexed in Scopus

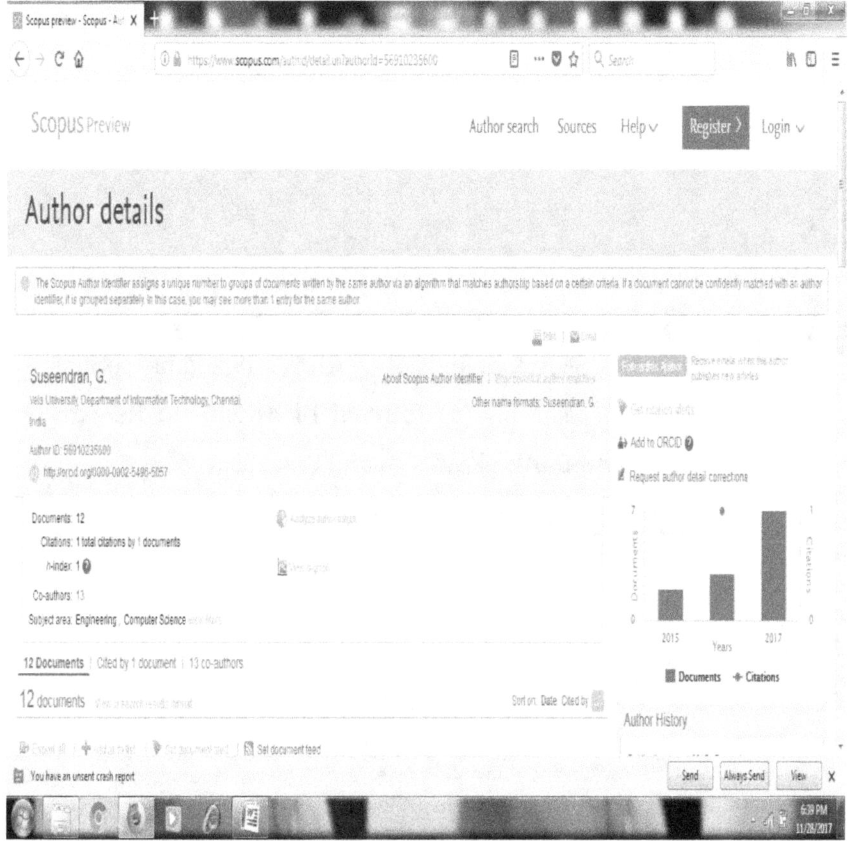

Searching Journal indexed in Scopus

1. Go to www.scopus.com.

2. Click Source from the top of the Screen.

3. It display a screen as below.

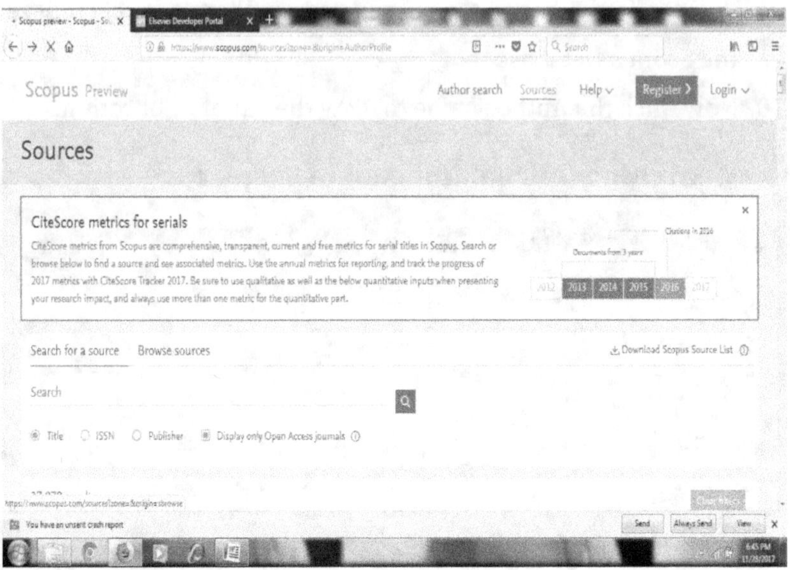

4. Click Search to Search of journal which is indexed in Scopus.

5. Enter the Journal Name as **Journal of Advanced Research in Dynamical and Control System** and Click Search.

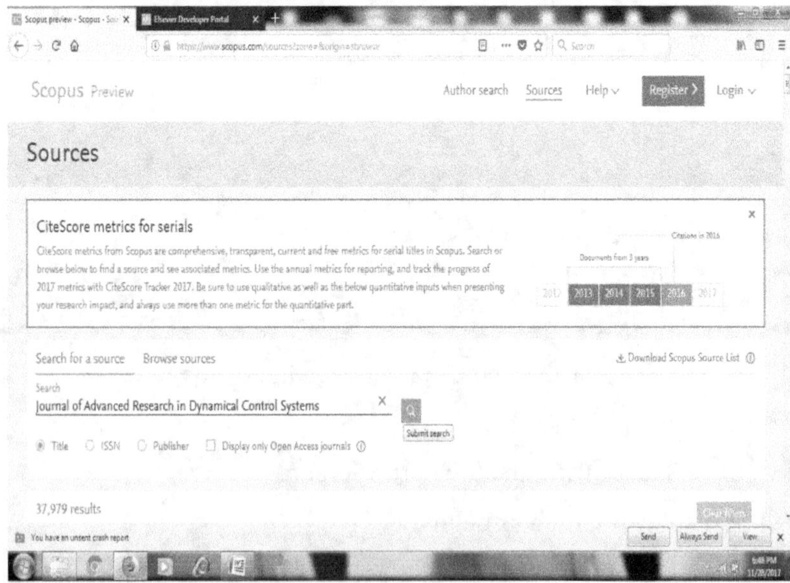

6. Click search button to search the Journal which is indexed in Scopus.

7. It display as below.

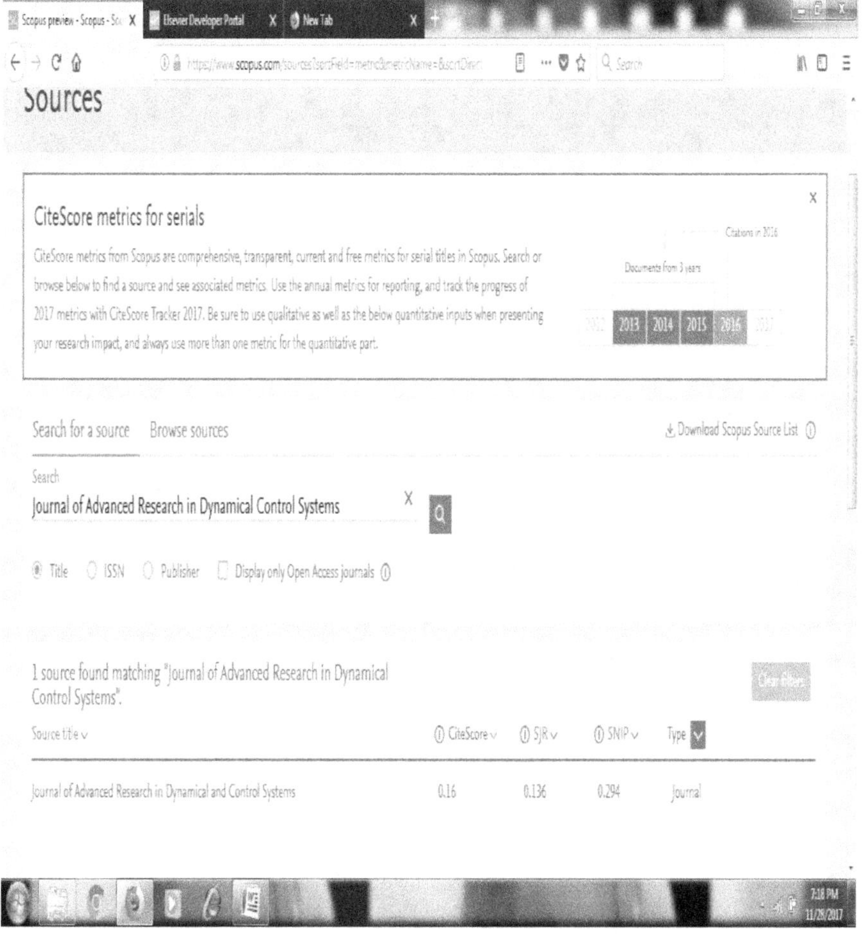

8. If the Journal is out of Scopus it displays **(Coverage period discontinued in Scopus).**

9. Enter the Journal name **Indian Journal of Science and Technology.**

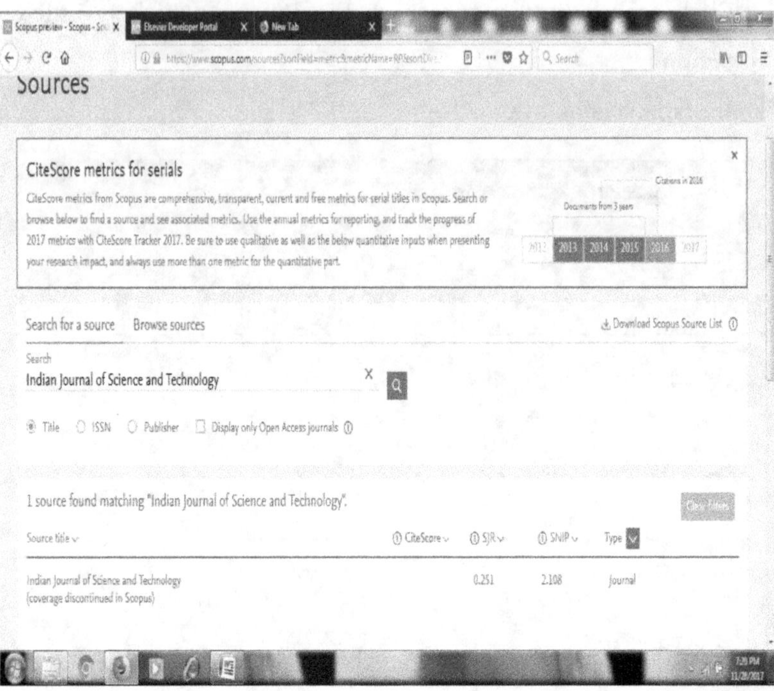
Sources
CiteScore metrics for serials
CiteScore metrics from Scopus are comprehensive, transparent, current and free metrics for serial titles in Scopus. Search or browse below to find a source and see associated metrics. Use the annual metrics for reporting, and track the progress of 2017 metrics with CiteScore Tracker 2017. Be sure to use qualitative as well as the below quantitative inputs when presenting your research impact, and always use more than one metric for the quantitative part.
Citations in 2016
Documents from 3 years
2012 2013 2014 2015 2016 2017
Search for a source   Browse sources
Download Scopus Source List
Search
Indian Journal of Science and Technology
Title   ISSN   Publisher   Display only Open Access journals
1 source found matching "Indian Journal of Science and Technology".
Clear filters
Source title   CiteScore   SJR   SNIP   Type
Indian Journal of Science and Technology   0.251   2.108   Journal
(coverage discontinued in Scopus)

www.ingramcontent.com/pod-product-compliance
Lightning Source LLC
LaVergne TN
LVHW041335200726
843509LV00009B/724